PRONOUNCING
ARABIC

I

PRONOUNCING
ARABIC
I

T.F. MITCHELL

CLARENDON PRESS · OXFORD

1990

Oxford University Press, Walton Street, Oxford OX2 6DP

Oxford New York Toronto
Delhi Bombay Calcutta Madras Karachi
Petaling Jaya Singapore Hong Kong Tokyo
Nairobi Dar es Salaam Cape Town
Melbourne Auckland

and associated companies in
Berlin Ibadan

Oxford is a trade mark of Oxford University Press

Published in the United States
by Oxford University Press, New York

British Library Cataloguing in Publication Data

Mitchell, T. F. (Terence Frederick), 1919–
Pronouncing Arabic 1.
1. Arabic language. Pronunciation
492'.7
ISBN 0-19-815151-9

Library of Congress Cataloging in Publication Data

Mitchell, T. F.
Pronouncing Arabic 1 / T. F. Mitchell.
Bibliography: p. Includes indexes.
1. Arabic language—Pronunciation. I. Title. II. Title:
Pronouncing Arabic one. III. Title: Pronouncing Arabic 1.
PJ6121.M58 1989   492'.7152—dc 19   88–15968
ISBN 0-19-815151-9

Set by Wyvern Typesetting Ltd

Printed and bound in Great Britain by
Courier International Ltd,
Tiptree, Essex

PREFACE

In *Writing Arabic*[1] reference was made to the forthcoming appearance of a companion volume on Arabic pronunciation. Thirty-five years later, this is that volume. Reasons for this notable delay are several, among them an earlier intention to publish in collaboration with the late J. R. Firth a rewritten version of W. H. T. Gairdner's *Phonetics of Arabic*,[2] the subsequent loss of the completed manuscript, which came posthumously to light among Professor Firth's papers, and my own translation from London to different fields of responsibility in Leeds. The need to fulfil the earlier promise was not, however, forgotten, and retirement has at last furnished the opportunity of redress. For the series of detaining 'accidents' I can only seek the understanding and indulgence of the reader, and do the little I can to make amends. In the mean time, I take the opportunity to pay long overdue tribute to Gairdner's early pioneering work.

T. F. M.

Lymington, 1987

[1] T. F. Mitchell, *Writing Arabic* (Oxford, OUP, 1953; paperback 1978).
[2] W. H. T. Gairdner, *The Phonetics of Arabic* (London, OUP, 1925).

ACKNOWLEDGEMENTS

I am indebted first and foremost to T. H. O. M. Dawood and A. R. Ayoub, stalwarts of the Egyptian 'Azhari' tradition, who, having come as students to the School of Oriental and African Studies in the period following the Second World War, first introduced me to the rigours of Arabic pronunciation. Their patience and tolerance in face of early unskilled efforts at imitation are still recalled with gratitude, and any surviving insufficiency is no fault of theirs. Regrettably, by reason of sheer numbers, the help and example of so many other Egyptian students and friends go individually unacknowledged, though I am no less conscious of how much I owe them. Among other willing helpers from the Arab world, my friend and colleague from Jordan, Shahir El-Hassan, will in particular discern the fruits of frequent colloquy, not least in Chapter 2.

Sincere thanks go, too, to Professor A. F. L. Beeston, who in many matters made his erudition freely accessible to me. Without his careful reading of the typescript, I should have strayed too often from the twin paths of tolerably clear exposition and Arabic linguistic propriety. Once again, remaining imperfections are mine alone. It should also be said that the phonemic transcription used is owed to Professor Beeston's valuable suggestion that, in order to make it as 'practical' as possible, it should be restricted to symbols available on the everyday typewriter. He will in numerous places recognize my further indebtedness.

It gives me great pleasure to acknowledge the unstintingly helpful and invariably friendly guidance of Anne Ashby and, more recently, Hilary Feldman and Jane Stuart-Smith of the Oxford University Press. I can only hope that the book merits the care they have devoted to it. I am also deeply grateful to John Waś and Enid Barker of the Press for the quite remarkable meticulousness with which they have read, corrected, and noticeably improved the typescript.

Finally, I am grateful to Longmans for their kind permission to draw freely upon material contained in the forthcoming *Handbook of English Pronunciation for Arabic Speakers*.

CONTENTS

ABBREVIATIONS AND SYMBOLS

The following conventions are used:

CA	Classical Arabic
MSA	Modern Standard Arabic
ESA	Educated Spoken Arabic
CARS	Classical Arabic reading style
IPA	International Phonetic Association
C	consonant
$C_1 \ldots C_2 \ldots$	first consonant . . . second consonant . . . of sequence
V	vowel
$V_1 \ldots V_2 \ldots$	first vowel . . . second vowel . . . of sequence
CC	consonant cluster
VV	long vowel
L	long (syllable)
Ƚ	not-long (syllable)
S	short (syllable)
Ƨ	not-short (syllable)
s.	singular
pl.	plural
m.	masculine
f.	feminine
accus.	accusative case
gen.	genitive case
obl.	oblique case
s.o.	someone
s.t.	something
*	precedes a form or pattern which is either unacceptable or hypothetical, and in Chapter 8, in Appendix A, section 2, and elsewhere, precedes a form which is variable as to accentuation. In 7.5 and

Appendix A, section 1, * follows a form which is pronounced with an omissible pausal vowel

´ marks the vowel of an accented syllable; intonationally, it indicates a rise of pitch in relation to preceding syllable(s)

` indicates falling tone

ˇ indicates falling–rising tone

− indicates level tone

↓ precedes a descent in pitch

↑ precedes a rise in pitch

/ separates contrasting or variant items or categories

√ precedes an Arabic root

[ ] encloses IPA-type transcription

♯ indicates variously zero or pause

± reads as 'with or without'

I

PRELIMINARIES

1.1 Object

Writing Arabic aimed to provide an acceptable model for writing the Arabic script. *Pronouncing Arabic I* is likewise normative, and aims to provide for imitation an acceptable mode of reading aloud a written Arabic text. The variety of reading 'accents' in the Arab world imposes both geographical restriction and the choice of a well-known, codified reading style. In view of the undeniable cultural and demographic dominance of Egypt, there can be no reasonable objection to the selection of an Egyptian accent, which not only is recognized and esteemed beyond the borders of Egypt but also conforms to an established code of orthoepy, in the traditional sense of 'correct' [*sic*] pronunciation of written forms. An orthoepic approach is adopted for purely practical reasons and does not imply acceptance of the widespread Arab view that written Arabic is alone worthy of study.

Even within such well-defined practice, however, permissible variation does occur in the reading style of educated Egyptians and is attributable to their regional origins and educational training as well as to the subject-matter that is read and the circumstances in which reading takes place. Written Arabic of a formal kind is broadly reducible to two varieties: on the one hand, the high Classical Arabic of ancient beginnings and Islamic liturgy, and, on the other, the more modern language of contemporary literature, journalism, news broadcasting, technological writing, administration, and diplomacy (so-called Modern Standard Arabic). Both varieties, CA and MSA, constitute the formal written language, and the pronunciation of MSA, let us say in the reading of news bulletins, departs relatively little in Egypt from that appropriate to the 'straightforward' reading of a liturgical text. CA and MSA, which mostly differ lexically, have both to be learned, and the reading of MSA, in contrast with CA, is sometimes subject to influence from the mother tongue, that is, the vernacular spoken language of the region (so-called 'colloquial', otherwise vernacular Arabic). This vernacular influence may well be noticed, for example, when a newspaper article is being read aloud, especially to a comparatively uneducated listener. Such departures from strict classical orthoepy, however, are few. It is with CA reading style (CARS) that this book is primarily concerned, and divergences between it and the style in which 'vernacular influence' appears will be specified as they arise and drawn together later in Appendix A.3. CARS is least subject to fluctuation, and the concordance between it and what may be regarded for practical purposes as its derivative is easily established. It also usefully provides a yardstick by which other 'accents' can be measured and compared. With the style of pronunciation on which the book is based thus defined, it must be emphasized that concern will *not* be with liturgical recitation and chant, nor with conversational Arabic of any kind, not even with that which occurs in the early, stiff stages of encounter between collocutors, when recourse is often had to the formal written language. Everyday educated Arabic speech of a conversational kind (Educated Spoken Arabic or ESA) is of a different phonetic, stylistic, and grammatical order, and demands a descriptive as opposed to a normative approach. Spoken Arabic proper will be the subject-matter of *Pronouncing Arabic II*. In the mean time, suffice it to say that the information and instructions as to pronunciation contained in the present book may be applied to the reading aloud of all genres of formal written Arabic.

1.2 General hints on pronunciation learning

In the course of the book instructions are given as to the pronunciation of individual sounds and words, and, more importantly, on how the latter are strung together in phrases and sentences. In very general terms, the student is asked to develop any skill he may possess in the art of mimicry. It will be found, even fairly early on, that learning by heart with the aid of an Arabic-speaking teacher just a few of the sentences in the book, or, better, some of the texts in *Writing Arabic* and in Appendix A, will help greatly, since it is surprising how little material is required to exhaust the phonetically difficult sequences of a language. The use of a recording device will be beneficial both in training the tongue to utter Arabic sounds and in sensitizing the ear to its sound discriminations. The intricacies of the processes involved should not be underestimated. When reading aloud, we use not only our eyes and articulatory apparatus but also our ears to monitor our spoken performance in what is clearly an activity of such complexity that constant practice will be necessary if fluency and accuracy are to be achieved. The learner should insist with an Arabic teacher on the need for patience and meticulous correction, then listen to and repeat each phrase and sentence over and over again, trying to recall every detail of pronunciation, including the rise and fall of the speaker's voice. He should also be on the look-out for hints and helps—for instance, the way in which Arabs pronounce English often provides a useful guide on Arabic features that have to be learned.

At the same time, the learner must beware of imposing his own speech habits on the language he is seeking to acquire. For example, since in the pronunciation of Classical Arabic the quality of vowels is carefully maintained, with any notable variation clearly defined in terms of consonantal context, vigilance on the part of the English speaker will be needed against his ingrained habit of reducing the vowels of so many unaccented syllables to a mixed, indeterminate quality, as in the case of the syllables following accented -to- in 'photógrapher', or, indeed, of sometimes eliminating them altogether, as in the first syllable of the same word. A word-by-word rendering of, say, 'at the back of the shop' would be more reminiscent of Arabic practice both rhythmically and qualitatively than the English reduction of 'at the' and 'of the'. Nor is it on such evident differences that learners should exclusively concentrate. It may not occur to them, for example, that post-accentual -th- following the short accented vowel of e.g. 'cátheter' is likely to be longer than the corresponding sound occurring pre-accentually in 'cathédral' and that any such post-accentual lengthening has to be guarded against when pronouncing, for instance, Arabic mátalan (ŧ = 'th') 'for example'. Not only is the difference between single and doubled or geminated consonants an important one in Arabic morphology but also, from a phonological and phonetic point of view, every Arabic syllable is clearly enunciated with its due quantitative weight. The pronunciation of Arabic kánaza 'he piled up, he amassed' is quite unlike that of English 'Cánada'. The three vowels of the Arabic word are for all practical purposes identical in quality, whereas the post-accentual second and third vowels of the English form are again reduced in quality and weight. The rhythmic

Kɜɛnədə

patterns of the two forms may be represented as ●●● versus ●••. These examples are cited in order to make the point that the learner must be prepared from the outset to unlearn some of his own long-standing, often deep-seated features of pronunciation and to adopt new habits in all relevant areas—consonant and vowel articulation, accentuation, intonation, and others.

1.3 Need for a phonetic frame of reference

It is not proposed that the student should be left to his own untutored efforts at imitation. He needs at least an outline framework of observation and reference both to sharpen up his performance in this or that respect and to enable him to talk to others intelligibly about matters in hand. A generally agreed framework eliminates an impressionistic, idiosyncratic response to pronunciation, and facilitates further study beyond the introductory stage. The need is met by the discipline of *phonetics*. Study is not taken far in this area, but the essential minimum is nevertheless provided for any serious and profitable study of pronunciation. We should at least be aware of the human mechanism of utterance and of what is involved from an articulatory standpoint in the acquisition of strange sounds. By the use of a knowledge of general phonatory processes we can learn or be taught to produce new sounds or to test several shades of sound until a suitable one becomes fixed in performance. The following chapter, therefore, gives a brief general account of our articulatory apparatus, and introduces some necessary terminology of a technical kind.

PHONETIC ESSENTIALS

2.1 Transcription

Speech sounds[1] are sounds capable of production by the organs we use for speech. They are distinguished from the units (and features) of the sound *system* of a given language or language variety. It is primarily for the representation of the latter that *phonetic transcription* is used in this book. It is of the type usually termed *phonemic*, as opposed to *narrow* transcription, in which additional symbols (generally those of the International Phonetic Association) are used to indicate greater detail of pronunciation. The phonemic transcription is a set of symbols of which each corresponds to a significant, usually word-distinguishing, consonant or vowel phoneme of Classical Arabic. In turn, each consonant or vowel phoneme corresponds to one symbol only of the transcription.[2] In fact, the relationship between the written letters of CA, including their diacritical indices, and their phonetic implications is so regular that a transcription is tantamount to a *transliteration*, that is, a letter-to-letter transfer from Arabic to roman shape, with an almost invariable correspondence between a significant Arabic sound and its written representation. This is in marked contrast with the facts of English spelling and orthoepy, as when, let us say, a single letter 'a' is pronounced in five different ways in 'pat, path, lathe, many, about',[3] or when the five vowel-letters of the English alphabet all sound alike in 'village, England, city, women, busy'. The Arabic learner is also largely spared the problems posed by the pronunci-

---

[1] Key terms in the chapter are italicized.

[2] A phonemic transcription is not the only kind that is used in phonological analysis, but it is inappropriate to discuss the theoretical basis of the several kinds in a book of this sort. It is sufficient to say that a phonemic transcription is well adapted to practical orthoepic purposes. Nevertheless, even in the pronunciation, i.e. reading aloud, of written Arabic, certain features, e.g. emphasis (pp. 27–30), which are ascribed to individual phoneme-letters, belong in fact to whole syllables or even longer stretches.

[3] At least in the so-called 'Received Pronunciation' associated, for instance, with radio and television newscasting.

ation within one word of the same vowel-letter with markedly
different values, in e.g. English 'eleven' or 'Morocco'. Although
the vagaries of English spelling are especially associated with
vowels, the consonant-letters, too, sometimes correspond in
random and un-Arabic fashion to the facts of pronunciation, as
when the initial sound of 'f' in 'five' occurs as 'ph-' in 'photograph'
and '-gh' in 'cough', or when 'th' occurs with different values in
'thin' and 'this'.

Fhin, zhis

2.2 The mechanism of utterance; consonants and vowels; phonetic terminology

Reference is deliberately made to the 'mechanism of utterance' in
preference to the 'organs of speech', since there are no organs for
which speech is the primary function. For example, we use for
normal speech purposes the *stream of air* or *column of air* which we
exhale from the lungs in breathing. Above the lungs is the *trachea* or
windpipe and in turn above it the *larynx*, the cartilaginous structure
housing the *vocal cords*, and these parts, too, have been developed
secondarily to meet the needs of phonation. The laryngeal casing
comprises three cartilages, the cricoid or ring cartilage which
supplies the base support for the system, the thyroid or shield
cartilage which, roughly <-shaped, takes at the front the form of a
prominent node commonly called the 'Adam's apple', and, finally,
the approximately triangular arytenoid cartilages at the rear. The
so-called vocal cords, which are in fact bands or folds of elastic
tissue running from front to rear of the larynx, are fixed to the
thyroid cartilage at the front and brought together or separated by
the rotatory action of the arytenoids at the rear. The supra-
laryngeal region, from larynx to lips, is sometimes termed the *vocal
tract*.

   In the pronunciation of *consonants*, the air-stream issuing from
the lungs and having passed through the larynx is either partially
obstructed or restricted in the case of *fricatives*, or completely
stopped momentarily somewhere along the vocal tract in the case of
stops or *plosives*.[1] In contrast, *vowels* are characterized by a free
passage of the air-stream. We can generally feel and describe

---

[1] The terms *stop* and *plosive* are often used more or less interchangeably. These
consonants typically comprise the three phases of onset, stop (i.e. closure of the air-
passage), and plosion (or release of the stop(ped air)).

bloks u whtrəvɛ

consonantal movements and postures between the active tongue and the relatively passive upper surfaces of the speech or vocal tract; for vowels, however, in the absence of closures and strictures, appeal must be made to auditory as well as articulatory means of perception and description. The ear is all-important for the purpose, and, more generally, speech must be seen as a matter of reception as well as production, so that ear-training is a vital part of pronunciation learning.

The aforementioned fricatives and plosives are described in terms of their (different) *manners of articulation*. (For the complementary *place of articulation*, see pp. 11 ff.) Though fricatives and plosives are the consonant classes containing most members, they are not the only possible consonantal types. *Affricates*, like initial j in jábal 'hill, mountain', or the initial and final consonants in English 'judge', combine plosion and friction as a consequence of the slow separation of the articulating organs. *Resonants* are characterized by relatively wide opening of the articulatory channel, and share other features with vowels. They include *nasals*, e.g. initial m and final n in man 'who', *laterals*, e.g. medial l in saláam 'peace', *trills* or *taps*, e.g. medial r in bard 'cold', and *semivowels*, e.g. initial w in wazn 'weight, measure', and initial y in yáabis 'dried up, desiccated'.

It is convenient to include at this point a diagram (Fig. 1) of the mechanism of utterance in order to facilitate reference to further constituent parts and to permit a more refined scheme of phonetic description.

There are three principal divisions of the organs which human beings have adapted for speech. These are:

1. The *respiratory system*, which provides the stream of air from the lungs which is used for the articulation and transmission of speech sounds. Relevant musculature is used for such purposes as variation of breath force and even in part syllabification. The air-stream passes via the tracheal passage, which is divided in the throat from the oesophagus or food-passage. We all know the discomfort occasioned by food or drink 'going down the wrong way', otherwise into the trachea instead of the oesophagus.

2. The *phonatory system* or larynx, containing first and foremost the vocal cords or bands, via which the air-stream typically passes. The space between the vocal cords is termed the *glottis*. The action

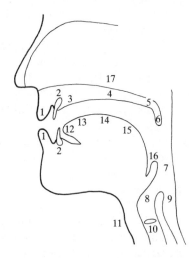

FIG. I. 1. Lip 2. Tooth 3. Alveolum 4. Hard palate 5. Soft palate 6. Uvula 7. Pharynx 8. Trachea 9. Oesophagus 10. Vocal cords 11. Adam's apple 12. Tongue-tip 13. Tongue-blade 14. Front of tongue 15. Back of tongue 16. Epiglottis 17. Nasal cavity

of the cords is at least fivefold, but three glottal states are greatly the most important (Fig. 2). Firstly, the cords may be held loosely together and made to vibrate[1] by the pressure of air from the lungs. This is the action of the cords for *voiced* sounds, as for all vowels and for, say, medial b in ṯábat 'he stood firm'. Secondly, they may be held wide apart, so that air passes through the glottis unimpeded. This is the glottal condition for *voiceless* sounds, such as initial t and final t in ṯábat.[2] Thirdly, the cords may be held tightly together, as when we fix the diaphragm prior to lifting a heavy weight. This third condition is that of the *glottal stop* (Arabic hamz).

The figure represents the cords vibrating for voice (i), wide apart for voicelessness (ii), tightly together for the glottal stop (iii). Less important vocal-cord activity includes very reduced opening to produce slight glottal friction in the pronunciation of h in e.g. hamz

---

[1] The movement is more accurately described as of periodic undulation. The rate of vibration may be varied in order to change voice *pitch*—the faster the rate, the higher the pitch.

[2] Stopping up the ears enables one easily to perceive the buzz of voicing as one passes, let us say, from voiceless s to voiced z: sss-zzz.

(i)   (ii)   (iii)

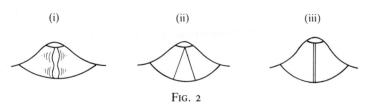

FIG. 2

'the glottal stop, glottalization'. If more breath force is used in order to produce some vibration of the vocal cords, then 'voiced h' occurs, as optionally in e.g. duhn 'oil'. Finally, it is possible to close the cords tightly and almost completely along their length, yet to allow passage of air through the cartilaginous material at their rear. The resultant rasping effect is that of one kind of whisper.

3. The supra-laryngeal *articulatory system*, which, comprising the cavities of the pharynx, the mouth, and the nose, together with such particular components as the palate and teeth and the active articulators of tongue and lips, is used to modify continuously the shape of the speech tract and thus to provide meaningful speech. The adjustable resonators of the system are principally the pharynx and the mouth. The overriding importance of activity within the mouth is recognized in detail at c below, and briefer consideration is first given at a and b to the functions of the pharyngal and nasal cavities.

a. The *pharyngal cavity* is the chamber extending from the back of the mouth and nose, in the rear of the *soft palate* or *velum*, to the place of division between trachea and oesophagus. The *epiglottis* or epiglottal fold is a cartilaginous flap folded around the extreme back or root of the tongue. It serves to protect the trachea, for example during swallowing. The epiglottis is fused with the root of the tongue and the whole drawn back and down towards the wall of the pharynx in the articulation of the characteristically Arabic pharyngal fricatives, initial and respectively voiceless and voiced in e.g. ḥubb 'love' and 9ayn 'eye; spring; letter 9ayn' (Fig. 3).

b. The *nasal cavity* provides a means of egress for the air-stream via the nose, access to which is provided or denied by the lowering or raising of the velum. Sounds during whose articulation the air passes through the nasal cavity are termed *nasal*, though the term is usually reserved for those sounds belonging to the sound *system* of a language. m and n are bilabial and (dento-)alveolar nasal con-

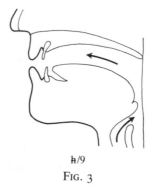

ħ/9

FIG. 3

sonants corresponding respectively to the voiced *oral* (= non-nasal) plosives b and d. The vowel in the word man 'who', however, occurring as it does between nasal consonants is *nasalized*, but, in contrast with, say, French, Arabic does not distinguish between oral and nasal vowel phonemes. Systematic use of nasalization is made in Quranic chant but this will not concern us. Arabic n is subject to variation in accordance with the place of articulation of a following consonant and this is particularly noticeable when this consonant is plosive. For example, n appears as a velar nasal (Fig. 5) before velar k in e.g. ?inkis@@r 'breaking, brokenness'. Articulation of this kind in which consonants share a given place of articulation is often termed *homorganic*, and n may be spoken of as a homorganic nasal consonant in association with a following plosive. Fig. 4 illustrates the difference in the position of the velum between oral (raised velum) and nasal (lowered velum) bilabial articulation, and Fig. 5 shows similar difference in the velar case.

c. The *oral* or *buccal cavity* is where most of the activity that concerns us takes place. The shape and volume of this cavity is primarily adjustable by the action of the highly flexible tongue, movable in its many muscular parts. The tongue's movement is to be seen in relation to the opposing faces of the vocal tract, whether these are immovable (*teeth*, *teeth-ridge* or *alveolum*, and *hard palate*) or subject to muscular innervation producing contraction and expansion (*soft palate*, *faucal* or *tonsillar arches*, and *pharynx*). The following sixfold division is according to articulators, active and passive, by far the most important of which is the tongue. At this point it is necessary to expand on the brief mention made (with

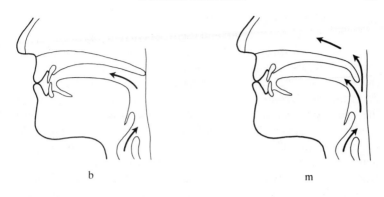

b   m

FIG. 4

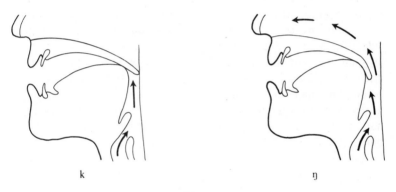

k   ŋ

FIG. 5

Note: ŋ is the IPA symbol for a velar nasal consonant.

reference to n under b above) of the second ordinate of consonant description, the *place of articulation*, to complement the earlier *manner of articulation* (i.e. as plosive, fricative, affricate, etc.). The pharyngal fricatives spoken of under a involved place as well as manner. The six divisions are as follows:

(i) *The teeth*. Sounds articulated between the tip (strictly, also the rim) of the tongue and the teeth are described as *dental*. Arabic t and d, among other consonants, have often been so described, but, since their articulation also involves some contact with the alveolum, they are better termed dento- or denti-alveolar (Fig. 6), as in wátad 'tent-peg'. The teeth are also involved in *labio-dental* articulation, i.e. between lip and teeth, as f in fam 'mouth' (Fig. 7).

(ii) *The teeth-ridge.* The teeth-ridge, also known as the alveolar ridge or, simply, the *alveolum*, is the area of the gums just behind the teeth. Sounds articulated between tongue and alveolum are described as *alveolar*, e.g. 'tapped' r in r@sm 'drawing' or b@r@d 'he filed' or ?amíir 'Emir'. English articulation has a general tendency towards alveolarity but, whereas English t/d, s/z, etc. are most frequently alveolar, similar Arabic sounds tend to contain a dental component of articulation. Nevertheless, the place of articulation can vary with neighbouring vowels, so that, at least in the case of some speakers, d in e.g. diin 'religion' is pronounced as alveolar in contrast with the dento-alveolar contact appropriate to daam 'it lasted, continued' or dam 'blood'.

(iii) *The hard palate.* This is the bony arch of the roof of the mouth. Sounds articulated between the front of the tongue and the hard palate are known as *palatal*, e.g. y in yamíin 'right hand, right side'. The name of the letter jiim is often pronounced by Egyptians as giim with an initial palatal plosive. The articulation of the affricate j, also of the fricatives ś as in śams 'sun' and ż, which, resembling the final consonant of English 'beige', often replaces j, typically involves the tongue and an area overlapping alveolum and hard palate. Such sounds are termed *palato-alveolar* as to their place of articulation (Fig. 8).

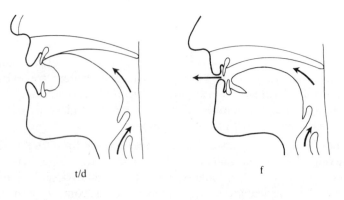

t/d	f
Fig. 6	Fig. 7

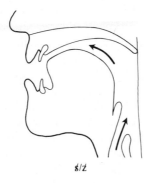

FIG. 8

(iv) *The soft palate.* The soft palate or velum is the soft, fleshy part at the rear of the roof of the mouth. The division between hard and soft palate can be felt with the tongue or finger. The soft palate can be raised or lowered, in the latter case to allow the stream of air access to the nasal cavity. Sounds articulated at the velum are termed *velar*, such as the velar plosive k in e.g. kátab 'he wrote' (Fig. 5). Also in Fig. 5, the velar contact and velar lowering are shown for a velar nasal consonant.

(v) *The uvula.* This is the small soft piece of flesh hanging down at the rear end of the velum between the tonsillar arches (Fig. 9). A consonantal sound articulated in this region is said to be *uvular*, a

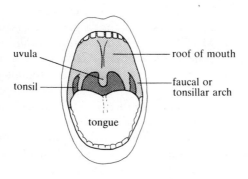

FIG. 9

voiceless uvular plosive in the case of q in e.g. q@@l 'he said', uvular fricatives, respectively voiceless and voiced, in the cases of x and ǵ, as in xubz 'bread', ǵ@rb 'west'. It should perhaps be said that the description of q in e.g. q@@l as a 'voiceless uvular plosive' leaves much unsaid, since, in fact, articulation also involves the upward movement of the trachea, the inward contraction of the faucal arches, and the complete filling of the pharynx by the root of the tongue, but description will not be pursued to this degree of detail.

(vi) *The tongue.* This is by far the most important articulator of speech sounds in the mouth. For descriptive purposes, the tongue is arbitrarily divided into the following five parts relative to the tongue's position of rest with its tip behind the lower teeth.

(*a*) The *tip*. This is the foremost part of the tongue, the extremity of the forward tapering section which also includes the *blade*. It should be distinguished from the all-round *rim* of the tongue.

(*b*) The *blade*. With the tip, the blade of the tongue normally lies opposite the alveolar ridge.

(c) The *front*. At rest this part of the tongue lies opposite the hard palate. It is raised towards the hard palate in the articulation of *front vowels*, e.g. those of tiin 'figs' and maat 'he died', and also in the articulation of certain consonants, e.g. palato-alveolar ʃ in ʃabáab 'youth'.

(*d*) The *back*. The back of the tongue at rest lies opposite the soft palate, towards which it is raised in the articulation of *back vowels*, such as u and uu in hunúud 'Indians' and @ and @@ in q@r@@r 'decision, resolution'. The back of the tongue and the soft palate are in contact in the case of the voiceless velar stop k (Fig. 5).

(*e*) The *centre*. This is the overlapping area between the front and the back. It is the central part of the tongue that is raised towards the palate in what are called *central vowels*. The unaccented vowels of English 'photographer' which were earlier termed 'mixed' or 'indeterminate' are, in phonetic terminology, central vowels. Vowels that are not fully front or back are often said to be *centralized*, which should not be confused with *central*. Arabic a and aa of saláam 'peace' are centralized vowels. The terms *fronted* and *backed* are similarly used of varieties of back and front vowels, and these terms are also sometimes used with reference to consonants, as when we talk of a front variety of k marked by simultaneous tongue contact with both hard and soft palates. This kind of variation commonly occurs in response to difference of surrounding vowels.

d. The *lips* also play a most important role as movable articulators in shaping the overall tract and thus affecting the nature of emitted sound. They may be shut tight, held closely or loosely together, or pursed and protruded. The closing and opening movement of the lower jaw, which controls the gap between upper and lower teeth, correlates with lip closing and opening. Both openings are close for fiil 'elephant', medium for baat 'he spent the night', and quite widely separated for T@@b 'it ripened'. Lip-position is particularly important for the quality of vowel sounds. When separated, the lips may also be *spread*, as for the vowel of fiil, *neutral*, as for the vowel of baat, or *rounded*, close-rounded as for the vowel of fuul 'beans' or with the slightest degree of rounding in the case of @ in T@yyib 'good, pleasant'. Though their position is especially relevant to vowel description, the lips are nevertheless also active in the pronunciation of consonants containing a *labial* component. Articulation may be *bilabial*, as in the case of b and m, or *labio-dental* as in that of f.

2.3 Vowels and the vowel figure; contrast between Arabic and English vowel systems

Not directly perceptible, not even by the 'feeling' with which we can know much concerning consonant articulation, the adjustments to the shape of the oral and pharyngal cavities performed by the tongue during the pronunciation of vowels require their own framework of classification and description. It is true that we can feel certain gross movements and postures of the tongue in the articulation of vowel sounds, that it is the front that is raised to produce the vowel of fii 'in' and that the tongue is flattened on the floor of the mouth with slight raising of the back in the interjection ?@@h 'Oh!' or for the vowel of n@@r 'fire'. The vowels, which can often be best perceived if whispered, should be isolated from the words in question both in general to practise the production and perception of vowels for their own sake and, in this case, to appreciate the articulatory difference between front and back. We can also use these vowel positions to demonstrate the difference between vowel and consonant, for if one starts from ii, for example, and raises the tongue a little further towards the hard palate, then the palatal friction appropriate to consonantal y is produced. Similarly, it is a short distance from the position for @@ to that for velar or even uvular friction. What is more, ii and @@ are vowels of clearly defined quality, as far as may be from the 'indeterminate', central quality spoken of earlier. However, although we can develop some general awareness of the articulatory difference between front (close) and back (open), we are unable by similar means to specify exactly the part of the tongue which is raised highest nor the degree of its raising, nor does this bare twofold distinction provide a means of accounting for the great wealth of vowel quality found in a given language.

In order to develop a more refined framework of description, we start from the aforementioned key positions of close front and open back, and, in relation to them, rely for further discrimination on largely auditory response, subsequently translated into articulatory terms, and supported by the direct observation of lip-position. A scheme of 'cardinal vowels' has been devised by first taking the fully close, fully front position (cardinal i) and the fully open, fully back position (cardinal ɑ), then lowering the tongue from i towards ɑ, and subsequently continuing the raising of the back of the tongue from ɑ towards the soft palate. Between i and ɑ, three intermediate positions have been selected, at approximately equal auditory intervals, later shown by radiography to be more or less equal in terms of tongue-raising also. These three intermediate values, for which the lips are spread or neutral, with greater spreading associated with closeness, are symbolized by e, ɛ, and a. i/e/ɛ/a comprise a close/half-close/half-open/open series. Similarly, three 'equidistant' points were found to continue the raising of the back of the tongue from cardinal ɑ, and to these additional cardinal values the symbols ɔ, o, and u were ascribed, so that u/o/ɔ/ɑ is a close-to-open back series corresponding to front i/e/ɛ/a. In the case of the back vowels, lip-position changes progressively from wide open for ɑ to close-rounded for u. It is possible to reverse the characteristic lip-positions for all these primary cardinal vowels and thereby produce noticeably different vowel quality, for example to round i or unround u, and, of course, all vowels may be nasal if the soft palate is lowered. We shall, however, refer in this book only to the eight primary oral values we have specified. In the past these values were often associated with 'key words' taken from well-known languages, such as the French of the Île de France or the German, let us say, of Hanover, e.g. i as in French *fit* 'he made', e as in French *fée* 'fairy', ɛ as in French *fait* 'he does', a as in French *mat* 'dull, matt', ɑ as in French *pas* 'step', ɔ as in German *Gott* 'God', o as in French *faux* 'false', u as in German *gut* 'good'. Although key-words are today discredited for the important reason among others that they are, in fact, pronounced in many different ways by speakers of a homogeneous language variety, they can nevertheless provide the beginner with a rough and ready guide which he can refine if he wishes by reference to recordings of the cardinal vowels that are obtainable from the Linguaphone Institute.

These eight clearly differentiated vowel qualities on the periphery of the oral area of vowel production can be plotted on a simplified diagram constructed in terms, firstly, of the part of the tongue which is raised highest, variously towards the hard palate (*front* vowels), the central palatal area (*central* vowels), or the soft palate (*back* vowels) and, secondly, of the height to which it is raised (*close/open* vowels, with intermediate subdivisions of *half-close* and *half-open*). The diagram or *vowel figure*, which may be imagined within the confines of the mouth, takes the form shown in Fig. 10. Additionally, in the description of vowels, reference must be made to lip-position (*spread/neutral/rounded*). Thus, i is described as a close front spread vowel, o as a half-close back rounded vowel, and ɛ as a half-open front vowel with lips neutrally open, or, more simply, a half-open front neutral vowel. Other vowel qualities may be plotted on the figure in relation to the cardinal values

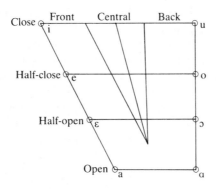

FIG. 10. The vowel figure

indicated and thereafter appropriately labelled. This will be done when the Arabic vowels are dealt with in detail in Chapter 5. On a practical level, there is much to be gained from developing a close awareness of a wide range of vowel sounds. This serves to speed up the acquisition of any unfamiliar vowel, for example aa[1] in Arabic laa 'no', by enabling the learner to locate its quality auditorily in relation to other qualities he already knows. It will be useful for present purposes to isolate the southern standard English vowels in, say, 'bead', 'bid', 'bed', 'bad', 'bud', 'card', 'cod', 'cawed', 'could', 'cooed', and 'curd'.

The eleven English vowel phonemes just illustrated underline the great contrast between the English and Arabic systems of vowel discriminations. Classical Arabic distinguishes only three vowel phonemes,[2] and these are not as a rule indicated in Arabic writing. The preceding pure vowels or monophthongs of English occur in both accented and unaccented syllables, and, in addition, there has to be reckoned the unaccented central vowel that is so prominent a feature of English. And there are yet more vowels, now of a diphthongal kind, to add to the overall English array. Diphthongal distinctions of the kind illustrated by 'laid', 'lied', 'Lloyd', 'lowed', and 'loud' are foreign to Arabic, where y and w following an open vowel, for example, are treated in CARS with the tenseness of articulation appropriate to consonants and not as the second elements of vowel-glides or diphthongs. There are other features affecting English vowels that must not be introduced into Arabic. Vowel length is the most important of these and is on a totally different footing in the two languages. The three vowels of Arabic are all subject to a short/long distinction (e.g. kátab 'he wrote'/ káatab 'he corresponded'), and length in relation to vowels behaves in a similar manner to gemination in relation to consonants. In southern standard English, however, some vowels are inherently long, for example those of 'seed' or 'saw', and others inherently short, for example those of 'sit' or 'cod'. Moreover, the length of long vowels varies in English in response to consonantal and other environmental features. Thus, the vowel of 'seed' is longer before the following voiced (better, lenis) consonant d than before the

---

[1] a(a) here does not symbolize the 'cardinal value' but rather one of the vowel phonemes of Arabic described in Chapter 5.

[2] But see also pp. 68–9.

voiceless (better, fortis) t in 'seat'.[1] Again, the vowel of 'seed', where no post-accentual syllable occurs, is longer than its counterpart in 'seeding'. More might be said about vowel length in English, but the sole concern here is to point out that such features again play no part in Arabic and must not be brought over to the pronunciation of the language. They too often are.

2.4 Prosodic features

There are important areas of pronunciation involving more than individual vowels and consonants. Outstanding among these are *accentuation*, *rhythm*, and *intonation*, and we shall say more on these subjects subsequently.[2] As a result of a combination of features, e.g. force of exhalation (*stress*) and pitch (*tone*), certain *syllables* stand out to the ear above others. We refer to such syllables as *prominent* or *accented*, like the first syllable of ħ@r@kah 'movement; vowel', the second of mufáttiš 'inspector', and the last of hirr@táan 'two cats'. In English, the incidence of the accent is unpredictable, having to be learned for individual words, whereas in Classical Arabic it is dependent upon the syllable structure of the total word-form. As to rhythm, we have already spoken of the need to avoid the English tendency to reduce the quantitative weight as well as the quality of unaccented vowels. At the same time, in both languages accented syllables tend to occur at roughly regular intervals of time. In Classical Arabic, however, this is much more closely linked to the word or phrase, since these elements are usually accented individually in the sentence. Finally, variation in the pitch of the voice occurs throughout the sentence and beyond. Rises and falls and sustained levels of pitch provide distinctive patterns of intonation. We shall see subsequently that, as far as Classical Arabic is concerned, all three of the areas we have singled out for mention are, as in English, closely interdependent.

2.5 Syllables and their types

Classical Arabic syllables are delimitable by the fact of their beginning with a consonant and containing a vocalic nucleus, as well as by the inadmissibility of syllable-initial clusters and of sequences

---

[1] For the lenis/fortis distinction, see p. 99.   [2] Chapters 7 and 8.

of more than two consonants. A glottal stop with a following vowel in support often occurs as a means of obviating the features of post-pausal vowel or consonant cluster, for example in the so-called derived forms vii–x of the verb, e.g. ?inkás@r 'it broke, was broken', ?iht@r@m 'he respected', ?ihm@rr 'he/it reddened, he blushed', ?istá9mal 'he used', where ?i- serves to obviate the initial clusters nk-, ht-, hm-, st-. This is the hamzátu lw@Sl or 'the hamzah of joining' (6.2), the name applied to the graphic representation of hamz, the glottal stop. The latter, together with the following vowel, is omitted when the preceding word ends in a vowel. ?a- of the article ?al- is also a case of w@Sl, and the name hamzátu lw@Sl itself illustrates the elision of ?a(lw@Sl).

Syllable structure is expressible in terms of C(onsonant) and V(owel). Vowels may occur short or long, and a long vowel may be symbolized by VV. Geminate and non-geminate consonant sequences and clusters may be distinguished notationally by the use of numerals, i.e. $-C_1C_1$ (geminate) and $-C_1C_2$ (non-geminate). Any syllable is derivable from the expression

$$CV(V)C_{0/1/2}$$

where the brackets enclose a potential increment of vowel length and zero indicates the non-occurrence of a final consonant in the structure of a syllable. If C_0 occurs, then the syllable is *open*, otherwise it is *closed*, the latter by means of one or two consonants at the terminal margin of the syllable. Sequences of more than two consonants are inadmissible, and when medial sequences of two consonants occur, each belongs by definition to a different syllable. Two-consonant clusters, geminate or non-geminate, occur only at the terminal margin of a single syllable that is final or pausal, and then as a consequence of the regular omission of pre-pausal short vowels, e.g. katábt for katábta 'you (s.m.) wrote'. As appeared in *Writing Arabic*, Arabic writing is a special kind of syllabary consisting mainly of consonants, and a consonant (h@rf) is said to be 'moved' (mutahárrik) if vowelled and 'resting' (sáakin or musák-kan) if not. The first consonant of two-consonant clusters is 'resting' or vowelless, in these terms, and the first component of a geminate consonant should be regarded similarly. It is this use of zero-vowel (sukúun) that prevents Arabic from consisting wholly of a series of open syllables, a form of patterning found in many of the world's languages, though not in English.

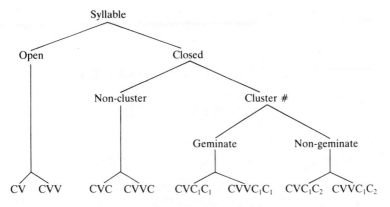

Note: the symbol # = pause

FIG. 11

The syllable types of Classical Arabic are as in Fig. 11. There are restrictions on the frequency and distribution of certain syllable types. The types CV, CVV, and CVC are least subject to distributional restriction, but we shall not concern ourselves here with questions of distribution. Exhaustive examples of the possible syllable patterns of words are given later with reference to accentuation.[1]

---

[1] Chapter 7.

THE ARABIC ALPHABET
PHONETICALLY
INTERPRETED

3.1 The alphabet and its roman transcription

The Arabic alphabet consists of twenty-eight consonants. These are listed at Table 1 in Arabic alphabetical order, together with the corresponding roman symbols employed in this book and the names of the letters in transcribed form.

There are numerous systems of roman letter-shapes for the transcription/transliteration of Arabic. In contrast with *Writing Arabic*, the transcription used here is based entirely on resources provided by an everyday typewriter. Capitals have been used for the Arabic 'emphatics', and, among diacritics, the hyphen and the solidus or oblique stroke have been used as part of certain letter-shapes.

The Classical Arabic vowels, fátḥah (a), kásr@h (i), and D@mmah (u), if they are included at all in a written text, appear as diacritics. When, however, length is applied to them, then three of the alphabetic shapes are used to symbolize it. Thus, 'long fátḥah' appears in the shape ‍ا or, under certain circumstances, ‍ى , 'long kásr@h' requires the use of ‍ى , and 'long D@mmah' that of ‍و . The symbol @ is used in the book to indicate a back open vowel (see pp. 68–9), but the non-phonemic distinction between a and @ is no part of Arabic writing.

A word should perhaps be said about the relationship between the transcription and the symbols of the International Phonetic Association, some of which appear elsewhere. IPA symbols are used where necessary to indicate greater detail of pronunciation in what is termed a 'narrow' transcription. Items (consonants, vowels, words) symbolized in this way are usually enclosed in square brackets. The phonemic symbols have a contextual rather than an individual value, that is to say that there is mutual dependence between them and other symbols of the context, for example

TABLE I

	Arabic	Roman	Name of letter
I	ا	aa/?	?álif/hámzah*
2	ب	b	baa?
3	ت	t	taa?
4	ث	ţ	ţaa? — *Fhaa*
5	ج	j	jiim
6	ح	ħ	ħaa? *xhaa*
7	خ	x	x@@?
8	د	d	daal
9	ذ	đ	đaal *zhaal*
10	ر	r	r@@?
11	ز	z	zaay
12	س	s	siin
13	ش	ś	śiin
14	ص	S	S@@d *lhaa*
15	ض	D	D@@d *jhaa thaa*
16	ط	T	T@@?
17	ظ	Ð	Ð@@?
18	ع	9	9ayn *gεyn dhaa*
19	غ	ǵ	ǵ@yn
20	ف	f	faa? *rheyn ghzzf*
21	ق	q	q@@f
22	ك	k	kaaf
23	ل	l	laam
24	م	m	miim
25	ن	n	nuun
26	ه	h	haa? *ghaa*
27	و	w	waaw
28	ى	y	yaa?

* Nowadays the term ?álif has a twofold implication: firstly the phonetic one of a long open vowel (aa), and secondly the written one of ا. Hámzah (ء) is the sign for the glottal stop and effectively the first consonant of the alphabet. It is not always associated with ?álif, but in certain contexts with waaw and yaa?, whereas, in other contexts again, it is written independently. It is, of course, written below ا when the vowel i follows. For the writing of hámzah, see *Writing Arabic*, pp. 20–1, 39–40, 79–81. The sign hámzah is the top of the letter 9ayn (no. 18). Its invention is attributed to the Arab grammarian Al-Khalil, whose regional origins may well explain the device, since in Iraq, Kuwait, and many parts of (Greater) Syria, the voiced pharyngal fricative is commonly glottalized or pronounced with a simultaneous glottal stop in words like 9ilm 'knowledge'. This is not part of Egyptian practice, nor of that of most Arab regions.

A. F. L. Beeston writes that 'up to and including the fourth century AD, ?alif always noted hamz and nothing else, while in the sixth and seventh centuries AD it was being used ambiguously either for hamz or for vowel-length: from the latter eighth century it ceased to be used by itself (and without the hamzah) as a consonantal letter'.

between the 'emphatic' consonants and neighbouring vowels and consonants, so that e.g. Đ in l@fĐ 'pronunciation' marks the whole word as the domain of 'emphasis'. 'Narrow' symbols, for their part, have a more restricted function and are used as a means of recording as far as possible or contextually necessary the shades and time-sequence of sounds. There is thus no theoretical limit to the 'narrowing' of transcription in explaining and amplifying the details of utterance. Those symbols of the transcription which differ from IPA usage are, in Arabic alphabetical order, as shown in Table 2.

TABLE 2

Transcription	IPA
?	ʔ
ŧ	θ
j	dʒ
ħ	ħ
x	χ
đ	ð
ś	ʃ
S	ʂ
D	ɖ
T	ţ
Đ (Z)*	ð(ẓ)
9	ʕ
ǵ	ʁ
y	j
@	ɑ

* See pp. 29–30.

3.2 Grouping of consonants by phonetic features

The Arabic alphabetic names are acrophonic, i.e. the name of each letter begins with its phonetic power, with the exception of ?álif, which does not now *by itself* note the sound of hamz. Likewise, hamzah, the sign for hamz, is not acrophonic. The main discernible principle in the conventional ordering of the letters is that ones distinguished from each other only by dots cluster together. Sporadic juxtapositions, in particular S/D/T/Đ, z/s/ś/S, q/k, m/n, w/ y, perhaps also t/ŧ and d/đ, nevertheless indicate some phonetic ordering.

Phonetic groupings proper are, of course, of a different kind. From the standpoint of place of articulation, the great majority of consonant sounds finding expression in the Arabic script fall in the dento-alveolar (t, T, d, D, ŧ, đ, Đ, s, S, z, (Z), r, l, n) and guttural, i.e. uvular/pharyngal/glottal (x, ġ, ħ, 9, ?, h; perhaps also q) zones of articulation. The remaining few are labial (f, b, m, w), palato-alveolar/palatal (š, j, y), and velar (k, (w)). (Table 3, p. 34) As to manner of articulation, three main types of correlation are distinguished in the script, voiced/non-voiced (= voiceless), emphatic/non-emphatic, and sulcal/non-sulcal. These are now considered in turn, and the point should be made in passing that the prefix 'non-' is not used here in a purely negative sense but indicates positive features of articulation.

(i) VOICED/VOICELESS

The wide separation of the vocal cords allowing unimpeded passage of air from the lungs is the glottal condition necessary for voiceless sounds. In contrast, glottal activity for voiced sounds requires the vocal cords to be drawn loosely together in such a way as to allow their forcing apart by the air-stream and their coming together again under their own elasticity. The undulating, voicing movement of the cords is usually referred to as 'the vibration of the vocal cords', though, strictly speaking, it is the column of air which vibrates in sympathy. Tests for the presence of voice are many. Mention has been made of stopping the ears when pronouncing, say, z(zz . . .). The buzz or hum ceases when the glottis is opened for s(ss . . .). Again, z(zz . . .) may be sung in contrast with s(ss . . .). Yet again, if the finger is pressed beneath the node of the Adam's apple, the vibration will be felt to cease on the passage from z(zz . . .) to s(ss . . .).

The voiced/voiceless feature is, of course, 'superimposed', so to speak, on distinctions otherwise mostly described in terms of place and manner of articulation. The voiced/voiceless correlative pairs of Classical Arabic consonants are as follows:

| *Voiced* | đ | d | z | D | ġ | 9 |
| *Voiceless* | ŧ | t | s | T | x | ħ |

Đ belongs to 'high Classical' style, appropriate, for example, to Quranic recitation, and is usually replaced elsewhere, even in the pronunciation of Classical Arabic, by Z. Z/S provide a further voiced/voiceless pairing. The usual Egyptian vernacular reflex of the voiced palato-alveolar affricate j is the voiced velar plosive g, often pronounced as a palatal plosive in the environment of a close front vowel (i or ii). As a *velar* plosive, g is the voiced correlative of k, but, though g may sometimes be heard for j in an Egyptian pronunciation of Classical Arabic, this is better avoided. Nevertheless, j has to be learned by Egyptians and others, and many speakers who are untrained in the classical tradition pronounce a voiced fricative $\dot{z}$ (pp. 12–13) in place of affricate j. In the case of such speakers, $\dot{z}/\dot{s}$ constitute a further (palato-alveolar fricative) pair of consonants differentiated in respect of the voiced/voiceless feature.

In spite of difference in both the manner of articulation (fricative as opposed to plosive) and place of articulation (labio-dental as opposed to bilabial), there are very good phonological grounds for the view that the voiced/voiceless correlation applies also to the labial pair b/f. For example, the occurrence of one member of any pair of the above six clearly differentiated correlatives excludes the occurrence of its partner within indigenous Arabic roots, for instance within the favourite structure $C_1VC_2VC_3$, and this exclusion also holds for b/f. The recognition of this close association of the labial pair makes for greater systematization among the consonants overall, as inspection of Table 3 will show.

Disregarding the imperfect voiced/voiceless relations b/f and j/$\dot{s}$, as well as the pair Z/S, we may say that k, q,[1] and h lack a voiced correlative, and that, conversely, no voiceless consonant phoneme corresponds to m, Ð, r, l, n, w, and y. ? cannot, by definition, be either voiced or voiceless.

We are at present considering, somewhat unrealistically, the pronunciation of consonants in isolation and deferring consideration of the implications of several kinds of junction. It should not be thought that what have been described as voiced and voiceless consonants necessarily remain so in all contexts. The contextually determined unvoicing of voiced consonants and voicing of voiceless consonants is dealt with in Chapter 6.

---

[1] In some dialects of Arabic, g appears as the reflex of CA q and then stands as the voiced velar plosive counterpart of voiceless k.

(II) EMPHATIC/NON-EMPHATIC

The grouping of consonants into voiced and voiceless correlatives is to be found in most if not all languages. Correlation between so-called 'emphatic' consonants and non-emphatic counterparts, however, is a noticeably Arabic feature. The articulatory processes involved must first and principally be seen in two dimensions as they concern the shape of the tongue; firstly, on a side view along its length, and secondly, on a front view across its width. The first dimension involves contrast between (i) the thrusting of the tongue forwards and upwards, with concomitant depressing of the back and opening of the pharyngal cavity, as in the pronunciation of a close front vowel but with the necessary further adjustments of the front of the tongue for the pronunciation of a dento-alveolar consonant (d, s, t, d), and (ii) the flattening of the tongue on the floor of the mouth as for an open back vowel, with perhaps minimal raising of the back, and with a corresponding reduction of the pharyngal cavity (Ð (Z), S, T, D). The difference may be roughly diagrammed as in Fig. 12.

The distinction thus outlined is in the main that between 'clear' (t) and 'dark' (T) articulation, which is most commonly made, for example in work on English pronunciation, between clear and dark varieties of the lateral resonant l, but the same difference is easily perceived between clear and dark d/Ð, s/S, t/T, and d/D, both during the articulatory 'hold' of the consonant and from the nature of any vocalic on- and off-glide to and from the hold-position. So much for the 'longitudinal' aspect of emphasis/non-emphasis, terms adopted, though they are not fully satisfactory, in preference to the use

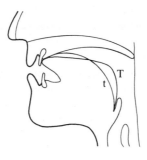

FIG. 12

elsewhere variously of velarization or pharyngalization in place of emphasis. Emphatic articulation has nothing to do with the raising of the back of the tongue towards the velum (velarization) and still less with the type of constriction associated with ħ and 9 and properly labelled pharyngal. It should be recalled that the use of 'non-' in non-emphatic or clear articulation betokens positive features of pronunciation. The second or 'latitudinal' dimension of the emphatic/non-emphatic difference marks it as clearly *sui generis* and sets it apart, at least as far as a strict Classical accent is concerned, from a simple clear/dark distinction. The tongue may not only be raised or lowered in its several parts but also laterally expanded or contracted along its length. The ancient Arab grammarians, the last section of whose works was devoted to the phonetics of the consonants, referred to emphasis as 'lidding' (?iTb@@q), and it seems plausible to believe that the reference was to the shape of a shallow dish (T@b@q) serving as an inverted lid or cover to the equally inverted container formed by the upper teeth and the palate. Such a description certainly fits emphatic articulation as it is taught in the Egyptian schools of Classical orthoepy.[1] The lateral expansion of the tongue along its length is of such a kind as to protrude the tongue between the upper and lower teeth, including the molars. The air between teeth and cheeks may in these circumstances be put under pressure and the cheeks puffed out, which is not possible if, as in the contrasting case of non-emphasis, the tongue is narrowed and withdrawn inside the confines of the teeth. The tongue is 'thin' and tense for the non-emphatics, 'thick' and lax, filling the mouth, so to speak, for the emphatics. The lips, too, play their part. Generally speaking, they are spread for the non-emphatics, neutral or slightly rounded for the emphatics. In the high Classical accent to which reference has been made, the lips are positively pursed and protruded as part of emphasis in e.g. Tiin 'clay, mud', ?@SSíin 'China', etc., but this should not be imitated for everyday purposes.

Though other groups distinguished in this chapter are not fully illustrated before Chapter 4, it has seemed appropriate to provide examples here of the comparatively unfamiliar emphatic/non-emphatic correlation. It has already been said that in Egypt, in

[1] For example, at Al-Azhar Mosque and University, and at Dār Al-'Ulūm, the teachers' training college in Cairo.

contrast with, say, Jordan or the Cyrenaican area of Libya, Ð
belongs only to high Classical style, and is elsewhere replaced by Z,
e.g. Ð@nn/Z@nn 'he thought', ħ@ÐÐ/ħ@ZZ 'luck', etc. Other
examples of the overall contrast are:[1]

t/T:

tiin 'figs'	Tiin 'clay, mud'
taab 'he repented'	T@@b 'it ripened; he got well'
tuub 'repent!'	Tuub 'bricks'
baat 'he spent the night'	ŝ@@T 'it (got) burnt'
bayt 'house'	ǵ@yT 'field'
sákat 'he fell silent'	s@q@T 'he fell'

d/D:

dall 'he directed'	D@ll 'he lost his way'
sa9d 'good luck'	b@9D 'some'
hádam 'he destroyed'	h@D@m 'he digested'
fáadi(n) 'redeemer'	f@@Di(n) 'empty, vacant'
m@rdúud 'returned, rejected'	m@rDúuD 'bruised'
y@rkud 'it becomes still'	y@rkuD 'he races away'

s/S:

sayf 'sword'	S@yf 'summer'
sáayil 'flowing, leaking'	S@@yil 'assaulting, having assaulted'
bass 'cat'	b@SS 'it shone'
q@ssáas 'slanderer'	q@SS@@S 'shearer'
nasíib 'relative, kinsman'	n@Síib 'share'
lams 'touching, handling'	l@mS 'railing at (s.o.)'

đ/Ð, z/Z:

đall 'he was humbled'	Ð@ll 'he continued (doing s.t.)'
đihn 'mind, intellect'	Ðuhr 'afternoon'
ħáđaf 'he cancelled, he erased'	ħ@f@Ð 'he kept, he looked after'

---

[1] Examples are as a rule given in their pause forms, i.e. final short vowels,
typically of nominal case, verbal mood (muD@@ri9), and past tense (m@@Dii), are
usually omitted, together with the final -n of indefiniteness. The feminine (táa?
m@rbúuT@h) endings -atun/-atan/-atin all appear as -ah. Pausal and non-pausal
forms are considered in detail in Chapter 6.

záahir 'shining, radiant'	Z@@hir (or Ð@@hir) 'clear, apparent'
ħazz 'he incised, he severed'	ħ@ZZ (or ħ@ÐÐ) 'luck'
ħáafiz 'incentive'	ħ@@fiZ (or ħ@@fiÐ)[1] 'guard'

Note. The fricative type (see sulcal/non-sulcal below) to which đ and Ð (also ŧ) belong is not only largely restricted to high Classical style[2] and to certain (particularly bedouin) dialects of Arabic but also, in general, occurs rarely in comparison with other articulatory types.

Though not all positions are exemplified in the foregoing lists, there is, in fact, no restriction on positional occurrence, so that emphatics and non-emphatics occur pre- and post-vocalically, pre- and post-consonantally, initially, medially, finally, and so on. We shall return to the general topic of (non-)emphasis when considering the relationship between consonants and vowel quality. In truth, (non-)emphasis belongs to syllables and even words as wholes and is only located in consonants for practical alphabetic, including phonemic, purposes.

The remaining consonant groups which we notice in this section require briefer treatment. They are the sulcal/non-sulcal group, the liquids, the gutturals, and the semivowels.

(III) SULCAL/NON-SULCAL

The articulatory difference between, for example, ŧ and s lies in the shape of the aperture through which air issues between the tip/blade of the tongue and the dento-alveolar region. The aperture in the case of ŧ, đ, and Ð is that of a slit, but in the case of s, S, z, and Z the shape is quasi-cylindrical as a result of the grooving or furrowing of the tongue. Viewed from the front, the difference may be represented diagrammatically as ⌢ (e.g. ŧ) as opposed to ⌵ (e.g. s). The term 'sulcal' is used to designate the latter type and 'non-sulcal' the former. Sulcal consonants are often termed sibilants. Non-sulcal articulation has, like the palato-alveolar affrication of j, to be consciously learned by most Arabs of urban origin, for example for the purpose of Quranic recitation and use in high Classical style. In vernacular Arabic, even as spoken by educated speakers, non-

---

[1] More strictly, ħaa-.
[2] It should not, however, be thought that the type does not occur within the wider scan of Educated Spoken Arabic.

sulcal articulation corresponds variously to sulcal and, more surprisingly, to *plosive* articulation, so that Ðúlma 'darkness' corresponds to both Zúlm@ and Egyptian vernacular D@lm@. This
correspondence may even occur within the same root, as when t, for
example, relates to s in musállas 'triangle' and samíin 'costly' but to
t in taláata 'three' and táman 'cost'. s is regularly the more educated
variant and the forms cited belong to more educated speech,
whereas those with t span a wider stylistic spectrum. For our present
Classical purposes, we shall use t in all such cases, i.e. mutállat,
taláatah, tamíin, táman. The contrastive pairs with which we are
concerned are t/s, ḍ/z, and the variants Ð and Z. S is not paired with
a non-sulcal counterpart.

(IV) 'LIQUIDS'

Liquids are a subgroup of what was earlier termed 'resonants'. The
term 'liquid' is not at all self-explanatory, even less than most, but a
label is needed not only to attach to the articulatory complemen-
tarity of trilled or tapped r (with (intermittent) opening along the
median line of the tongue, closure between the sides of the tongue
and palate) and lateral l (median closure, lateral opening), but also,
perhaps more importantly, to anticipate the bringing together of
these consonants and n (full dento-alveolar closure, nasal opening),
since all three behave as a group in the constituency of Arabic roots
(see 3.4). Articulatory difference between l and r may be diagrammed roughly as in Fig. 13. We return to these and all other

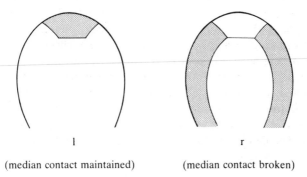

l
r

(median contact maintained)   (median contact broken)

FIG. 13. Plan-view of tongue–palate contact

consonants in Chapter 4 and Appendix A, where they are fully exemplified.

(V) GUTTURALS

Attention under this heading is drawn to the 'throat' consonants x, ġ, ħ, 9, h, and ?. Like the liquids and other groups we shall distinguish in 3.4, the gutturals behave as a group in terms of the (in)compatibility of its members within Arabic roots. There is also, for instance, a noticeable tendency for these consonants to be associated with open rather than close vowels, though the fact stands out more clearly in vernacular than in Classical Arabic. Nevertheless, there is a strong tendency even in CA for the consonants to occur with the vowel a in preference to i or u as the conjugational vowel of the imperfect (or non-past) tense. There are, therefore, substantial reasons for considering them as a group, quite apart from the overall zone of articulation which they share.

(VI) SEMIVOWELS

Finally, we should notice the semivowels w and y, which, though treated as consonants from an articulatory standpoint in Classical Arabic, none the less behave in their own way. Not only are the letters representing them used in written Arabic also to manifest long vowels, but, at least in vernacular Arabic, they are indeed often pronounced as vowels. Similarly, the CA sequences aw and ay often correspond to pure vowels (mid,[1] back and front) in vernacular. Again, as so-called 'weak' radicals, their morphophonological behaviour sets them apart from all other consonants except ? in all varieties of the language. Nevertheless, the Arabic semivowels do not behave wholly in the manner of English counterparts in, say, 'wet' and 'yet'. English semivowels are very short, weakly articulated close back (u) and front (i) vowels, from which positions the tongue moves rapidly to that of a following more prominent vowel providing the syllable nucleus. Semivowels, for their part, occur only at the syllable margin, and for this reason are generally classified as consonants, though they are vocalic in purely phonetic terms. The label 'semivowel' has been retained for Arabic w and y,

---

[1] The term 'mid' is often usefully employed either to designate a degree of tongue-raising for vowels between half-open and half-close (see Fig. 10 and pp. 16–17) or to cover an area of raising encompassing both grades.

but their articulation, at least in Classical pronunciation, involves more forceful, consonantal-type articulation than the corresponding sounds in English. Details are provided in the following chapter (p. 61 ff.).

3.3 Zone and manner of consonant articulation

It will be useful at this point to reorder the consonants as presented in Table 1 of 3.1 in the light of what has been said in 3.2. Table 3 presents the consonants in terms of their manner and place of articulation, though 'zone' has been preferred to 'place' as a means of indicating the spread to which consonantal articulation is subject in accordance with contextual features, not least appertaining to surrounding vowels. Following Table 3, we shall briefly discuss the manner of referring to the complexes of phonetic features subsumed by the consonant symbols. Although non-emphasis/ emphasis belongs, strictly speaking, to the vertical ordinate of *manner*, convenience of tabulation has dictated its inclusion along the horizontal ordinate of *zone* or *place*. This also has the advantage of locating the feature fairly and squarely within the dento-alveolar zone. The round brackets in the table enclose common variants, (g) and (ź) of j, (Z) of Ð. The square bracket in the case of [w] indicates that the semivowel comprises both labial and velar components. w is, of course, described as *labio-velar*.

When conventionally labelling a given consonant, one first cites any relevant voiceless/voiced distinction, follows this by the zone of articulation, including any non-emphatic/emphatic feature in the dento-alveolar zone, and concludes with the manner of articulation preceded by any non-sulcal/sulcal difference. Thus, b is labelled 'a voiced (bi)labial stop', t 'a voiceless dento-alveolar non-emphatic stop', S 'a voiceless dento-alveolar emphatic sulcal fricative', and so on. Where no voiceless/voiced, non-emphatic/emphatic, non-sulcal/sulcal correlation is indicated, then zone and manner will suffice, e.g. h 'a glottal fricative', n 'a dento-alveolar nasal', etc. The terms 'resonant' and 'liquid' are omitted, so that r, for example, is simply 'an alveolar tapped or trilled consonant'. Geminate rr consists typically of a series of intermittent taps forming a trill. The tap/trill difference is pertinent especially to intervocalic occurrence.

TABLE 3

Manner of Articulation		Labial	Dento-Alveolar Non-emphatic	Dento-Alveolar Emphatic	Palato-Alveolar and palatal	Velar	Uvular	Pharyngal	Glottal
Zone of Articulation									
Stop or Plosive	Voiceless		t	T		k	q		ʔ
	Voiced	b	d	D		(g)			
Fricative	Voiceless	f					x	ħ	h
	Voiced						ġ	9	
Non-Sulcal	Voiceless		t						
	Voiced		đ	Đ					
Sulcal	Voiceless		s	S	ś				
	Voiced		z	(Z)	(ż)				
Affricate	Voiced				j				
Liquid	Trill		r						
	Lateral		l						
	Nasal	m	n						
Semivowel		w			y	[w]			

The descriptive label attached to a particular consonant is not derived from some imagined scheme of universal phonetic categories but, at least in part, from contrasts developed with other consonants in Arabic pronunciation and word-formation (see 3.4). t, for example, is often described as 'a voiceless dental plosive', but this is inadequate, not only because 'dental' is misleading as opposed to 'dento-alveolar'[1] but also because of the relationship in which t stands with T, i.e. of non-emphatic to emphatic. To label t unequivocally, it should be said to be 'a voiceless dento-alveolar non-emphatic stop (or plosive)'. Similarly, to describe t as 'a voiceless interdental fricative'—and this is often done—is sketchy and again misleading. The label 'a voiceless dento-alveolar non-sulcal fricative' should be preferred.

3.4 Compatibility and incompatibility of consonants and consonant features

Arabic consonants do not freely combine within indigenous roots. In unaffixed forms and the favourite tri-radical root, consonantal compatibility/incompatibility is partly due to 'distance' between articulatory zones and partly to a relationship of exclusion or not between consonant features. There are essentially four zones, the labio-dental extending from the lips to the cutting edges of the teeth, the dento-alveolar from the teeth to the front of the hard palate behind the alveolum, the palatal from the front of the hard palate to the velum, and the guttural rearwards from the velum. A given consonant assembles several features, so that ḍ, for example, is dento-alveolar as to zone, but is also voiced, non-emphatic, non-sulcal, and fricative, and each of these features has its own implications as to what may or may not accompany it within a root. In addition, consonant groups differ as to their general productivity. The non-sulcals (t, ḍ, Ð) are the least productive group, whereas the most productive, capable of association with any other group, is that of the liquids (r, l, n). Incompatibility of consonants, on the

---

[1] Notwithstanding some variation in the place of tongue contact in response to e.g. difference of surrounding vowels, contact for t is typically made by the tongue both with the teeth (or junction of teeth and gums) and with the gingival or alveolar region. This contact usually involves the rim of the tongue and the whole teeth-cage, not simply the tongue-tip and the front teeth.

other hand, tends to be a function of their similarity, whether as to zone or by reason of any or all of the features which they muster.

The domain of (in)compatibility is subdivisible into immediate successions of radical consonants (C_1-C_2 and C_2-C_3) on the one hand, and interrupted successions (C_1-C_3) on the other. Duplication of consonants with interposed vowel is common only at C_2-C_3, e.g. 9ádad 'number', sábab 'reason, cause', S@ḥíiḥ 'true', etc., and in principle implies the occurrence of geminated clustering of the consonants elsewhere in the paradigm of related forms, e.g. 9ádad 'number', 9add 'he counted', etc.[1] Duplication does occur at C_1-C_3, e.g. ṭáaliṭ 'third' (ordinal adjective), q@l@q 'apprehension, worry', but this is rare, and no duplicates occur at C_1-C_2. In the greatly more frequent non-duplicate contexts, as a result of constraints on mutual accompaniment, the twenty-eight consonants of Classical Arabic do not all co-occur freely within roots. A radical consonant is subject to constraints imposed by any following and/or preceding radical. To take the voiceless/voiced correlation, for example, it can be said that, with the exception of the imperfect palato-alveolar pair š/(ž) (<j) (cf. the forms šáž@r 'trees' and žayš 'army' corresponding to the recommended šáj@r and jayš), any voiced member of a correlative pair excludes its voiceless counterpart in all domains, and vice versa. wátad 'tent-peg', drawn from rural and bedouin usage, is a single exception. It is the incompatibility that obtains as much between f and b as any other voiceless/voiced pair that strongly suggests that the labio-dental and bilabial articulatory difference should be disregarded and f paired with b in terms of the voiceless/voiced correlation. The labio-velar semivowel (w) occurs with labiality proper (f, b, m) in an adjoining consonant place, e.g. w@fq 'sufficiency; harmony', mawt 'death', 9afw 'elimination; forgiveness', and membership of the group is defined by the incompatibility of f, b, and m. Exclusion obtains not only between labio-dental friction and bilabial plosion but also between either of these and bilabial nasality, so that if m and f or m and b occupy successive places, then the form in question is certainly morphologically complex, arising from

---

[1] 'Duplication' of single consonants should not be confused with the 'reduplication' of bilateral roots, e.g. ġ@rġ@r 'he gargled'.

prefixal m- and radical f or b, e.g. mufállas 'bankrupt', mablúul 'wet(ted)'.[1]

In the dento-alveolar zone, it is plosives and (sulcal) fricatives that combine most freely. Non-sulcal and sulcal fricatives mutually repel, so that, for example, đ may not co-occur with s, S, z, (Z). Since đ is excluded from co-occurrence with Đ by the non-emphasis/emphasis constraint, and with t by the voiceless/voiced constraint, đ is incompatible with t, Đ, s, S, z, (Z). More generally, since similar incompatibility obtains among the remaining fricatives, it can be said that dento-alveolar friction may occur only once.

Within the liquid group, r and l co-occur only in that order and in the interrupted succession C_1-C_3, which suggests that they are the most like within the threefold group that also includes nasal n. Order of occurrence does seem to be of some importance, though the facts are less clear than those of (in)compatibility. The liquids have by far the highest frequency of occurrence of all consonants, n as C_1, r then l as C_2 and C_3. This in itself suggests the need to recognize the group, apart from the articulatory resemblances to which reference has already been made, but it is the fact of much incompatibility that clearly justifies the grouping. Liquid successions do occur at C_2-C_3, e.g. q@rn 'century; horn', but by no means all associations that are prima facie possible are in fact exploited, and n does not occur as C_2 in such successions. The most striking fact is that 'liquidity' may occur only once in the domain C_1-C_2, so that loan-words are at once recognizable as such from any infringement of this rule, e.g. vernacular Jordanian lurd 'Lord' or lanj 'brand-new'.

As to gutturals, though e.g. 9ahd 'promise', x@da9 'he deceived' are among rare exceptions, there is a strong tendency for guttural friction (x, ǵ, ħ, 9, h) to occur only once within roots.

The account of (in)compatibility might be greatly extended, but enough indication has now been given of the restrictions which operate at any given place within indigenous Arabic roots to put the phonemic discrimination of twenty-eight consonants in proper perspective. It is time now to turn to more practical problems concerning the pronunciation of the consonants.

---

[1] An exception belonging to the exceptional noun class of parts of the body is fam 'mouth', which is unusual both for the sequence f-m and for its overall structure CVC, usually reserved for the particle class and for certain weak verb forms.

4

HINTS ON THE PRONUNCIATION OF THE CONSONANTS

This chapter is concerned with the pronunciation of consonants presented within familiar groups (4.1(i)–(vi)) and the gemination or doubling of consonants (4.2).

4.1 Pronunciation of consonants by groups

(i) LABIALS (f, b, m)

f: As f in English 'film, duffer, riff-raff'. Arabic fiil 'elephant', dáfan 'he buried; concealed', x@fíif 'light' (adj.). The sound is frequently voiced (as v in English 'river') when it precedes a voiced pre-pausal dento-alveolar consonant, especially of the fricative category, e.g. l@fÐ (pronounced l@vÐ or l@vZ) 'pronunciation'. This assimilation for voice does not occur before consonants from other articulatory zones, e.g. daf9 'repelling', 9afw 'forgiveness'.

b: Again formed as its English counterpart. Arabic pronunciation is characterized by its vigour, at least among male speakers,[1] and all consonants, including b, are pronounced with greater muscular tension than in English. An English tendency to unvoice voiced consonants in initial position, to pronounce even a weakly articulated p for b, should be resisted, though the stricture applies less to final position, where unvoicing occurs in both Arabic and English (see 6.3). Though Quranic recitation is not our objective, it is of interest to note that final unvoicing offends in this style and that voicing is ensured by the inclusion of a final short vocalic off-glide of central quality, as in baabᵓ 'door; chapter' (see Note on q@lq@lah, p. 44). The frequent vernacular unvoicing of b before voiceless consonants (especially dento-alveolars) should also be resisted for

---

[1] Women's speech, consciously 'delicate and light', is characterized by such further features as a noticeable de-emphasizing of emphatic consonants, a closing of open vowel quality (so-called ?imáalah), etc., some of which can occur in their pronunciation of Classical Arabic.

Classical purposes, e.g. sabt 'sabbath, Saturday', kabs 'pressure, pressing'. Where it is felt necessary to refer to the feature of unvoicing, IPA transcription uses a small circle, usually subscript as in the examples quoted, i.e. saḅt, kaḅs, superscript in the case of a descending letter, e.g. j̊. Further examples of b are baat 'he spent the night', ḥabs 'obstructing; imprisonment', náa?ib 'representative, deputy', kalb 'dog'.

m: Again as in English but with greater muscular tension at the lips. Once again, final unvoicing occurs, especially after voiceless consonants, e.g. qism 'part, portion; department', but is on the whole better avoided in Classical pronunciation. Unlike the dento-alveolar nasal n, m is not subject to homorganic articulation with following consonants (pp. 10, 50–1). Although the range of forms taken by homorganically articulated n includes that of a bilabial nasal, e.g. jamb (<janb) 'side', nevertheless there is no real overlap between the two nasals in the consonant system. Related forms at once reveal the constituency of a given root, cf. plural junúub, ?ajnáab 'sides', and, in any case, as was seen in 3.4, a labial sequence -mb is inadmissible within roots. Examples of m are mawt 'death', jámal 'camel', samn 'clarified butter', šatm 'cursing; abuse', fam 'mouth'.

(II) DENTO-ALVEOLARS

(a) fricatives and plosives (t ḍ Ḍ; t d T D; s z S (Z))

t ḍ: Non-sulcal fricatives, respectively voiceless and voiced, both non-emphatic. Pronunciation is approximately as in English 'theme' (t) and 'these' (ḍ). These English examples have been expressly chosen with a close front vowel following t and ḍ in order to ensure 'clear' articulation of the consonant. Both consonants should be imbued with an ii-like resonance, since both are non-emphatic, notwithstanding the absence of any emphatic correlative of t. They are, of course, at the same time non-sulcal in contrast with sulcal s and z. As in all non-emphatic articulation, the tongue is well within the confines of the upper teeth, and a mirror may be used to practise the lateral contraction/expansion of the tongue appropriate to non-emphasis/emphasis. The front of the tongue is, of course, raised and the back depressed, much as for an ii-vowel, and the lips are spread. We shall later contrast these features with emphatic Ḍ. See also pp. 27–30. Examples of t and ḍ are tumma 'then', ?át@r 'trace', mitl 'resemblance, similarity', baɤt 'sending (out); resurrection', batt 'spreading', dawabáan 'melting', háadaa 'this' (s.m.), kidb 'lying, deceiving', m@qdúuf 'missile, projectile', ladáa?id 'pleasures, delights'.

Ð: The emphatic correlative of d and, in the absence of voiced/ voiceless correlation, also of t. All three non-sulcal consonants belong to high Classical style, and, in the field of vernacular Arabic, to rural and bedouin dialects. In educated urban CA, Ð is typically replaced by Z, whose non-emphatic correlate is, of course, z. Again, the mirror may be used to practise the lateral (emphatic) expansion and (non-emphatic) contraction of the tongue, with simultaneous relaxing and 'thickening' of the tongue for Ð. These features of Ð, indeed of all the emphatics, are perceptible especially in those parts of the tongue in the region of the molars. When laterally expanding or broadening the tongue, the object should be to touch the cheeks with its sides. It may help, too, to hollow the tongue behind the tip, positioning the tongue as for the vowel of southern standard English 'hot' or Arabic T@@b 'it ripened', keeping the front low in the mouth and the jaw sufficiently open to facilitate observation in the mirror, then turning the tip and blade upwards in the direction of the upper lip. This hollowing should be felt in the blade and rearwards. The best advice, however, is to close the air-passage in the dento-alveolar region, imagining that one is going to pronounce an open back vowel of the aforementioned kind, and then puffing out the cheeks. The sides of the tongue will be felt between the molars and it is this posture that is required for the fully emphatic consonants of high Classical style. There is, of course, no need to puff the cheeks out while pronouncing them, but this is the best means of developing tactile awareness of the tongue action involved. Although it is easier to start as suggested with complete closure at the front end of the oral cavity, the air between teeth and cheeks can be put under some pressure even when allowed to escape during the fricative articulation of e.g. Ð. It is when the tongue is held within the confines of the upper teeth, or when, say, the jaws are held wide apart as for an open back vowel, that it is physically impossible to put 'cheek air' under pressure. Strictly speaking, the usual simple description of tongue posture as front-raised (non-emphatic) or back-raised (emphatic) is inadequate not only for the description of fully emphatic consonants but also for accompanying vowels, since it does not embrace the abovementioned inter-molar activity of the tongue. It suffices, however, for practical purposes, since the 'emphatics proper' belong, at least in Egypt and the Levant, and more generally away from bedouin usage, only to high Classical style. In the spoken Arabic of many Egyptians, for example, a straight-forward front/back contrast corresponds to the non-emphatic/emphatic distinction of Classical tajwíid or Quranic orthoepy.

The low, 'dark' resonance of the emphatics contrasts with the clear-cut, 'high frequency' character of corresponding non-emphatics. It is usually helpful early on to pre-voice Ð, that is, to introduce the buzz of voice from the onset of friction, even leng-thening the sound in the process, and to compare the resonance with that obtained from the pre-voicing of ḍ. Similarly, the quality of on- and off-glides is a useful test. Compare in this respect, let us say, laḍíiḍ [-iːðˈ]¹ 'delicious' and ḥ@ÐíiÐ [-iːˀðˈˀ]² 'lucky'. Further detail of the quality of vowels accompanying emphatics and non-emphatics is given in Chapter 5. Lip-position is also important. The emphatics are associated with neutral lips, and, in high Classical style, even with rounding and protrusion, whereas the non-emphatics are characterized by lip-spreading. Examples of Ð: Ðulm 'injustice', 9@Ðíim 'mighty' (s.m.), m@Ðlúum 'wronged' (s.m.), ?@9Ð@m 'mightier', ?@fÐ@@Ð 'crude, coarse' (pl.). For exam-ples of the contrast between ḍ and Ð (Z), see p. 29.

t d: Although these consonants are subject to minor variation as to place of articulation in response especially to difference of neighbouring vowels, the variation may be ignored and is negligible in comparison with the roughly similar sounds of English. For example, the tongue–teeth (dental) contact for English t and d before ŧ in 'eighth', 'width', the alveolar contact for 'tea' and 'deem', and the post-alveolar contact for 'tree' and 'dream' cover a range of tongue position beyond anything that obtains in Arabic. The Arabic sounds are dento-alveolar in principle, involving simultaneous contact with teeth and alveolum, whereas the most frequent English type is alveolar only. The implication of this is that the English-speaking learner is well advised to aim at a *dental* pronunciation akin to that of, say, French *thé*, *dé*, etc. The tongue-tip may be up or down, that is to say that the front contact with the

---

¹ ɪ is an IPA symbol for a half-close front spread vowel; ː following i symbolizes length.

² ə represents, of course, a central vowel.

teeth may be made by the tip or the blade, with the rim firmly against the inside of the teeth all round. The learner should at first ensure that the tip touches the cutting edge of the front teeth and that the blade is in contact with the teeth up to and beyond the gums.

The same remarks concerning the non-emphatic/emphatic, clear/dark contrast apply to t and T, d and D as have been made already for đ and Đ. The clearness of t and d can be cultivated by concentrating on the similar quality occurring between close and half-close front vowels in English 'meaty' and 'seedy'. Otherwise, start with the vowel ii and move on to a dento-alveolar t/d, retaining, as far as allowed by the articulation of the consonant, the tongue position of the vowel. Then release the closure, still keeping the tongue in position for an ii-vowel, so that the off-glide also has the resonance of a close front vowel. Contrast in this way, for example, mabíit [-iːtˡ] 'overnight stay' with muḥíiT [-iːᵊtᵊ] 'ocean'.

Another relevant area of difference between English and Arabic is that of *aspiration*. The English voiceless plosives (p, t, k), especially when they are initial in an accented syllable, are strongly *aspirated*, that is to say that between the release of the stop and a following vowel there occurs a puff of breath or aspiration (p^h, t^h, k^h). This feature is absent following sibilant s in the clusters sp-, st-, sk-. Contrast in this respect the pairs 'p^har/spar', 't^heam/steam', 'c^horn/scorn'. Although Arabic t (and k) are slightly aspirated in similar contexts, the aspiration is so slight in comparison with English that the learner should pronounce the Arabic consonant as in his unaspirated st- (sk-) context. The vowel must begin immediately on release of the consonant, and it may help to be thinking of the vowel during the stop phase before release. It may also be found useful to practise while holding the breath in order to prevent the unwanted puff on release. Holding the breath, however, typically involves closing the glottis, and care must be taken to ensure that no unwanted glottal stop is produced on release of t- (or k-). Voiceless stops are noticeably less aspirated in some English dialects, for example those of Yorkshire, and the learner could find help from such sources.

The release of t and d in e.g. English 'button' and 'middle' is typically made without the occurrence of a vowel between the stop and the nasal, i.e. -tn, or between the stop and the lateral, i.e. -dl. The opening of the nasal cavity in the former case and of the oral cavity (by lowering the sides of the tongue) in the second case are respectively termed *nasal plosion* and *lateral plosion*. These forms of release do not give rise to problems for Arabic pronunciation, in which they also occur, e.g. fatn 'enticing away', ladn 'gentle; flexible', fatl 'entwining', 9adl 'straightforwardness; justice'.

T D: It is unnecessary to repeat what has already been said concerning emphatic articulation with reference to Ð. The plosives, however, probably offer the best means of developing control over the lateral movement of the tongue in relation to the molars. The tongue should be placed in firm contact with the upper teeth and teeth-ridge all round, and at the back should 'spill over' between the molars. As with t and d, the tip may be down but is typically up, with articulation effected by both tip and blade. The names of the consonant letters (T@@?, D@@?), as with all the emphatics, pro-vide good examples for practice. If the articulatory type is mastered before the back open vowel of such examples and articulation maintained in other vocalic contexts, then the appropriate vowel glides will, so to speak, look after themselves, as in mafíiD [-iː°ɖ°] 'drain; way out' in contrast with mufíid [-iːdʲ] 'useful'. It may again be helpful to pre-voice initial d and D, to imbue the onset of dall 'he showed', for example, with the quality of a half-close front vowel [ɪ] in contrast with the central to back resonance appropriate to D@ll 'he continued'.

As with t, so with T there is no aspiration of the plosive before a following vowel, which must begin immediately after release of the stop. Nasal and lateral plosion also occur with the emphatics as with their non-emphatic counterparts, e.g. b@Tn 'stomach', ǧ@Dn 'fold, crease', r@Tl 'rotl',[1] f@Dl 'surplus; graciousness'.

In vernacular Arabic, as a result of the consonantal and vocalic context, a mid-grade may be heard between non-emphatic and emphatic. This occurs most commonly in the context of open vowels and r. In Egypt, for example, the three grades as they concern d and D may be heard in dars 'lesson', d@rb (the mid-grade) 'path', and D@rb 'hitting'. Mid-grade examples may also occur in Classical pronunciation, for instance in x@dd@r 'he anaesthetized', which contrasts minimally with x@DD@r 'he tilled'. Vernacular habits may be taken over into Classical pronunciation by those who have

---

[1] A weight whose value varies according to country; approximately 1 lb. avoirdupois in Egypt.

not been schooled in the strict Classical tradition. By and large, the twofold distinction of non-emphatic/emphatic pronunciation is maintained, though now and then some confusion as to spelling arises, and sometimes, too, in response to questioning, one may be told 'It is really daal but it sounds like D@@d', when the mid-grade has occurred.

Note on q@lq@lah *and* D@@d

For purposes of Quranic recitation, T@@? is treated in the same way as b before pause, that is, it is released with a central vocalic off-glide, the purpose of which is held to be the full *voicing* of the consonant. A similar vowel is required to be pronounced after d, j, and q, and though the feature is understandable enough in relation to *voiced* b, d, j, it is puzzling to find it also applied to *voiceless* T and q. b, d, j, T, and q are known as ?alħurúufu lmuq@lq@lah and the feature itself as q@lq@lah. The omission of D from the list is also a puzzle. Reflexes of T in regional dialects are often noteworthy—in Upper Egypt, in the Al-Karnak dialect of Qena, for example, it seems to occur as a 'click'[1] with simultaneous dento-alveolar and uvular closure. In Berber, a non-Arabic language widely spoken in North Africa and increasingly as one moves westwards, the gemination of voiced D often takes the form of voiceless TT. Vernacular forms of Arabic share many features with Berber. The ancient Arabs declared themselves to be the people who 'speak with D@@d', called Arabic 'the D@@d language', and denied to all foreigners the capacity to pronounce D@@d, but it may be that T@@? should also have claimed their attention. The pronunciation of D@@d they referred to appears to have involved both lateral articulation and friction—in the form of either a lateral fricative or affricate—as well as emphasis. Nothing resembling this description of D@@d occurs in the Arabic-speaking world today, though I once heard what was presumably an imitation of it from a sheikh belonging to a non-Arab Islamic community of Zanzibar.

Examples of t, d, T, and D are tibn 'straw', fáatin 'tempting', fítnah 'temptation', maftúuħ 'opened' (s.m.), nabáat 'plants, vegetation', dáfan 'he buried', q@dam 'foot; step', tabdíil 'change, alteration', jild 'skin', ?ábad 'eternity', T@bíib 'doctor', m@T@r 'rain', ?@Tfáal 'infants', ?@mT@@r 'rains', ǵ@yT 'field', D@r@b

---

[1] 'Clicks' are characterized by double closure at the velum (or uvula) and further forward on the palate. Pulling the tongue back has the effect of rarefying the air between the closures, so that on release an ingression of air takes place in contrast with the normal egression of speech. Clicks are significant sounds in languages of southern Africa (Zulu, Hottentot, Bushman), and occur in English as interjections, notably the reproof usually written 'tut-tut' and the encouraging 'tsk-tsk' used to make a horse 'gee up'.

'he hit', f@Díilah 'excellence', ǵ@Dbáan 'angry' (s.m.), m@qDúuD 'perforated' (s.m.), ?@by@D 'white' (s.m.). For further examples, specifically of t/T, d/D contrast, see p. 29.

s z: These are non-emphatic sulcal consonants and the most noticeable difference between them and their English counterparts is that in Arabic the hiss is of higher frequency, much more clear-cut.[1] Pronounce an s and z with, as far as possible, the tongue position of a close front vowel and with lips vigorously spread. The upper lip should be lifted slightly from the upper teeth.

S (Z): Again, the low resonance of the emphatics is perhaps at its most noticeable with the sulcals, for which, in their emphatic form, instructions are as for Đ, T, and D. Lip position is again important. Instead of non-emphatic spreading, the lips are neutral or slightly rounded. Exaggerated lip-protrusion in the early stages should help to produce the 'dark' resonance required. In contrast with s and z, little muscular tension is felt in the lips or tongue for S (and Z).

Mid-grades between s and S, z and Z, occur as with the other non-emphatic/emphatic pairs, and particular care will be needed in order to pronounce certain examples of s with an acceptable Classical pronunciation. It will be necessary, for example, to distinguish clearly between sáf@r 'departure' and S@f@r 'jaundice; emptiness', and to make the more difficult contrast between f@r@s 'mare' and b@r@S 'leprosy', where the vocalic context is more closely similar. It should not be thought that it is surrounding vowel quality that distinguishes emphatic from non-emphatic consonants. It is rather the consonants that determine the quality of vowels or even other consonants, frequently at some remove. With common words like basíiT 'small, trifling', mabsúuT 'content, happy' (s.m.), some speakers feel it to be pedantic to pronounce them as indicated and prefer (the vernacular) b@SíiT and m@bSúuT.

Examples of s, z, S: saláam 'peace', násaj 'he wove, knitted', r@sm 'drawing', lams 'touching', faas 'Fez' (in Morocco), safr 'sighing', 9azíiz 'mighty; cherished', ǵ@zl 'spinning', karz 'preaching' (the Gospel), baaz 'falcon', Sulb 'firm, rigid', r@S@@S 'lead; bullets', ?@Sl 'origin', fúrS@h 'opportunity; vacation', x@@liS 'pure, unadulterated'.

For examples of Z and the z/Z contrast, see p. 30.

---

[1] As Gairdner observed, our 'hiss' is so weak and indeterminate that native speakers of Arabic often hear it as a lisping ŧ rather than sibilant s.

(b) liquids (r l n)

r: The defining characteristic of Arabic r is the tapping of the tip of the tongue against the alveolum. It is thus like the r of Scottish English and quite unlike the so-called 'frictionless continuant' of most parts of England as well as the retroflex r of the south-west and, more generally, rural England, parts of Lancashire, Ireland, and most of the United States, not to mention the uvular r of north-eastern England, which resembles that of northern France and Germany. The Scottish r of 'rum', 'borough', 'firm', 'fear', etc., is what is required in the pronunciation of Arabic r@dd 'he returned; returning', j@r@@ 'it flowed', f@rm 'chopping fine', ?amíir 'prince'. Arabic ?amíir sounds nothing like the typical English pronunciation of 'a mere'. It will be seen from this example and also from f@rm that it will not only be necessary for most students to work at acquiring a suitable pronunciation of r but they will also need to learn to pronounce Arabic r wherever it occurs, whatever the context. In particular, it must be pronounced before a consonant, e.g. bard 'cold', and when final, e.g. n@@r 'fire', which is in marked contrast with the typical southern standard English pronunciation of e.g. 'farm', 'far', etc., where r of the spelling does not correspond to any consonant sound in pronunciation.

The Arabic examples quoted above are of a single tap, but a rapid succession of taps make up a trill or roll, and r is trilled when geminated or doubled (by regular morphological process) and often, though optionally, when non-geminated r occurs after a consonant and before pause. Examples of obligatorily trilled r are q@rr@b 'he brought near' and m@q@rr 'habitation', whereas bi?r 'well' illustrates an optional trill. With these should be contrasted the contexts of single-tap occurrence illustrated by, say, r@ml 'sand' (initial), b@r@kah 'blessing' (intervocalic, non-geminated), b@rq 'lightning' (pre-consonantal), kás@r 'he broke' (post-vocalic, pre-pausal), t@qríir 'report' (the first r post-consonantal but syllable-initial, the second r again post-vocalic and pre-pausal). q@rr@r 'he decided' is an example of trilled and one-tap r in the same word.

One-tap r is relatively easy to acquire. Many English speakers use it already in intervocalic position following an accented syllable in words like 'very', 'thorough', etc., and also after t in e.g. 'through'.

Those who do not use it habitually in these contexts may acquire it by pronouncing d very rapidly in the foregoing English words, or by practising the 'flipping' of the tip of the tongue against the teeth-ridge from the tongue's position of rest in the mouth. Tongue–palate contact for d and tapped r is very similar, differing principally in the lightness and rapidity of the contact made for r at the front centre of the teeth-ridge in contrast with the firm all-round contact for d. In the case of r, too, there is firm side-contact at least at the molars. The similarity between d and tapped r informs a well-known exercise designed to teach tapped r. This is to pronounce English nonsense syllables of the kind gədɑ: or tədɑ: (rhyming with, say, 'tra-la') with gradually increasing speed. The usual result of rapid acceleration is a one-tap r in grɑ:, trɑ:. The sound may then be isolated and practised further by inserting it into English words of varying structure.

Trilled or rolled r offers greater difficulty to those unable to produce it by imitation. The starting-point is the one-tap r, since trilled r is an intermittent succession of such taps, with regular making and breaking of contact at the teeth-ridge. From the starting-point of the tapped r, and with the tip of the tongue as relaxed as possible, the jaw should be opened fairly wide and the opening then reduced with a simultaneous 'launch' of the tongue-tip at the alveolum in order to make the tip vibrate. As the jaw opening is reduced, it can be felt that the sides of the tongue come into firm contact with the molars and the rear part of the teeth-ridge. Early practice is likely to produce a rather breathy succession of two or three taps, whereafter further practice will be needed to control the sound with or without surrounding vowels of differing qualities. It may well be found easier at first to make a *voiceless* trill, and the suggestion implicit in the earlier instructions of first practising the sound following a fairly open vowel (say, that of southern standard English 'but') is also likely to help. This is simply a pronunciation hint, and it should perhaps be added that any tendency for opener vowels to accompany trilled rr is less noticeable in Arabic than in e.g. Spanish, where the first vowel of, for instance, *perro* 'dog' is opener than that of *pero* 'but'.

When r is final, a preceding vowel, such as ii in ?amíir, must be held until the very moment that the tap for r is made. It is also necessary, it should be recalled, to pronounce r clearly before and after a consonant, as in q@rn 'horn; century', badr 'full moon'.

Before pause, post-consonantal r, as in the last example, is often unvoiced (bad̥r).

In Egyptian vernacular Arabic, 'clear' and 'dark' varieties of r, accompanied in particular by respectively front and back varieties of the open vowel, are regularly distinguished. For example, b@rd 'filing' differs in this way from bard 'cold', b@rr@ 'outside' from wárra 'he showed', etc. In some structures the distinction between the vowels a and i following r implies a back/front difference in an open vowel preceding r, e.g. ḥ@@r@b 'he waged war against' as opposed to ḥáaris 'guard', muḥ@@r@bah 'combating' as opposed to madaarísa 'schools' (obl.). Such differences are often carried over into Classical pronunciation.[1]

Examples of r and rr: r@?s 'head', fáaris 'horseman', f@rš̥ 'furnishings, furniture', maḥr@mah 'handkerchief', ?áḥm@r 'red' (s.m.), murúur 'passing, passage; traffic', ?@rr@ml 'the sand', f@rr@@š̥ 'servant', sirr 'secret', murr 'bitter' (s.m.), m@@rr 'passer-by, pedestrian'.

l: This is a lateral consonant, so termed because one or, more usually, both sides of the tongue is/are lowered to allow the passage of air while median contact is maintained with the dento-alveolar region of the palate. The lowering of the side(s) is easily perceived in the pronunciation of, say, English 'little' or 'middle', which are examples of so-called *lateral plosion*, i.e. of the lateral release of the stops t and d.

l-sounds take on the timbres of as many vowels as require different shapes of the tongue and lips but are divisible for practical purposes into the two familiar 'clear' and 'dark' varieties, the former with the front of the tongue raised and the back depressed, the latter with the tongue flattened and perhaps some raising of the back. To this difference may be added that of non-emphasis/emphasis, since in some contexts l is emphatic; that is, of course, to say that the tongue is 'broadened' (or laterally expanded) and 'thickened' in contrast with the contraction and 'thinning' of non-emphasis.

The greatest learning difficulty will be presented by the typical clearness of Arabic l in contexts where, in most varieties of British

---

[1] muḥ@@r@bah would typically occur in spoken Arabic with a back vowel in the final syllable, i.e. muḥ@@r@b@, and in Classical pronunciation it may be this vowel only which is fronted; in strict accordance with tajwíid an open front vowel should also succeed ḥ, i.e. *muḥaar@bah.

and American English, a dark l regularly occurs.[1] In Irish English, especially in Eire, the clear l that is wanted occurs in all positions, including final and pre-consonantal, as in 'feel' and 'field', where the great majority of speakers of British English typically use a dark l. On the other hand, clear l *is* used before vowels in British English, except notably in most of Scotland, and it is a comparatively easy matter to lengthen and isolate the l of, say, 'leave' and thereafter to learn to use this kind of l in Arabic. The word 'leave' is chosen because the lateral is here followed by a close front vowel, the resonance of which should inform Arabic l. If difficulty is experienced, adopting the posture for l and then trying to pronounce ii *at the same time* should help. This is probably a simpler stratagem than the alternative of starting with the ii-position and then retaining it as far as possible while taking up the posture of the lateral consonant.

The substitution of dark for clear l offends the Arab ear, perhaps mainly because of the special association of darkness (and emphasis) with the name of 'Allah'. Most Americans and Scots, in particular, need to pay special attention to the matter, since they regularly use dark l in all contexts, even pre-vocalically as in 'leave', 'please', etc. Welsh speakers, on the other hand, though tending to use varieties of l that are not as clear as in the southern Irish case, will encounter fewer problems. The American habit of eliminating l altogether before the following palatal semivowel in e.g. 'million' should, of course, be avoided at all costs (cf. Arabic malyáan 'full').

Once the learner has acquired the ability to produce a clear l in isolation, he will need to practise it in different combinations, after different vowels as well as pre-consonantally and finally, as in falt 'escaping from', q@lb 'heart', milk 'property', mulk 'rule, sovereignty', ?@Tfáal 'infants', burtuq@@l 'orange', tamtíil 'citation, exemplification', duxúul 'entry'. Any tendency to substitute for l a vowel of the type that occurs in southern English 'put'—a widespread speech habit in London, the home counties, and elsewhere—must be strongly resisted.

Final, post-consonantal l is frequently unvoiced, especially after voiceless consonants, e.g. r@Tḷ 'pound', f@Sḷ 'severance; chapter; article', buxḷ 'avarice'. The last phase of the consonant is also often unvoiced in final post-vocalic position, e.g. naḥḥáalḷ 'bee-keeper',

---

[1] The darkest variety is typically that associated with lateral plosion.

and the final removal of the tip from dento-alveolar contact may be made audibly. (For final unvoicing in general, see 6.3.)

The only word in which *emphatic* l is acknowledged to occur by Arabic speakers is the divine name ?@ll@@h 'Allah, God', but, since the 'spread' of emphasis often covers successions of consonants and even whole syllables and successions of syllables, emphatic or at least dark l also occurs frequently elsewhere, as in f@Dl 'surplus; graciousness', xilT 'ingredient', l@fÐ 'pronunciation', b@lT@h 'axe', b@rT@l 'he bribed'. A careful Classical rendering requires, for example, the pronunciation T@lab 'he searched for; he asked for', but vernacular, mother-tongue habits die hard and T@l@b may well be heard. Since it is only in the divine name that l is positively emphatic, it has not been considered necessary to use a separate symbol for l in this context—the darkness of the form is indicated where appropriate by writing @ rather than a. The tenet of the Islamic creed 'There is no god but God' provides good practice in the pronunciation of clear and dark l and associated vowels, i.e. láa ?iláaha ?íll@ ll@@h. ?@l- of ?@ll@@h is derivationally the article, from which ?@- is regularly omitted after a vowel. When this vowel is the open vowel, as in the preceding example, or when it is the back rounded vowel u, as in r@ḥmátu ll@@h 'the mercy of God', then l is dark (and usually emphatic) and -@@- is back, but after the front spread vowel i, l is clear and -aa- is front, as in bí smi lláah 'in the name of God'. The example is one of 'vowel harmony', a feature much more widespread in vernacular than in Classical Arabic.[1]

n: For practical purposes, as English n. The consonant is, however, homorganically articulated with a following plosive, as a bilabial nasal [m] before b, e.g. danb [-mb] 'sin, crime', as a velar nasal [ŋ][2] before k and g, e.g. D@nk [-ŋk] 'poverty, distress', sankári(i) 'tinsmith', ?ingiltír@(@)[3] 'England', as a uvular nasal [N] before q, e.g. x@nq [-Nq] 'strangulation', minq@@r 'beak, bill'. Similarly, the contact made for n is palato-alveolar before palato-alveolar š and j, e.g. winš 'winch, derrick', ?ifr@nji(i) 'European'. Homorganic articulation of n sometimes also occurs before other fricatives, for example labio-dental [ɱ] before labio-dental f, e.g.

---

[1] See, however, pp. 96–7.
[2] As -ng in southern English 'sing'.
[3] Notice the regular occurrence of g in this borrowed geographical term. These terms are often *sui generis* as to pronunciation and other features.

?anf 'nose',[1] but this pronunciation is better avoided for Classical purposes.

Like r, l, m, and many other consonants, n may occur voiceless in final, post-consonantal position, especially after a voiceless consonant, e.g. b@Tn̥ 'stomach'. (See also pp. 38–9, 48, and 49–50, and 6.3.)

(III) PALATO-ALVEOLARS (ś, j)

ś: A voiceless palato-alveolar fricative for which the tongue-tip is drawn a little further back than for s and the front of the tongue raised higher. It corresponds to English sh of 'sheep', but care must always be taken to keep ś 'clear' whatever the context, since dark varieties of the corresponding English sound do occur. This instruction as to clearness applies equally to the voiced correlative ż, which sometimes occurs as the reflex of j in Classical pronunciation, and also to j itself.

Examples of ś: śakl 'likeness; shape', ?aśádd 'stronger', ruśd 'integrity; good sense', b@qśiiś 'tip, gratuity', r@śś 'sprinkling, watering', r@śśáaś 'hose; machine-gun'.

j: A voiced palato-alveolar affricate, corresponding to English j in 'jeep'. This pronunciation, as in jaríidah 'newspaper', is high Classical, and is thus distributionally restricted among spoken variants. It is commonly replaced by g (as in English 'go', and the voiced correlative of k) by speakers from Cairo and other parts of Lower Egypt, and the replacement may be heard in their rendering of Classical Arabic. For Egyptians in general, both j and ż, which sometimes replaces j, have to be learned. j combines the sounds of d and ż, the fricative component resulting from the slowly performed release of the stop. It is not surprising, therefore, to find that in the vernacular Arabic of Upper Egypt, palato-alveolar j corresponds to a palatal affricate [ɟ], which combines features of a fronted g and an off-glide in the form of y. From among the variants mentioned, the learner is recommended to adopt j for Classical purposes, though he should be aware of the restriction on its use. j, like ś (and ż), is always associated with 'clear' articulation.

Examples of j: jayś 'army', śáj@r@h 'tree', ?ájlas 'he sat s.o. down, made s.o. sit down', sijn 'prison', must@xr@j 'extract, excerpt'.

---

[1] As typical m in English 'symphony'.

(IV) VELAR/UVULAR PLOSIVES (k, q)

k: A voiceless velar plosive, as k in English 'king', 'cool', etc. Mention has been made of a voiced correlative g as a variant of j and also occurring in such non-Arabic geographical names as ?ingiltír@(@) 'England'. As in English, the place of velar contact varies in proportion to difference of surrounding vowels. If one takes up the k-position for, let us say, English 'key', and, without pronouncing the following vowel, changes one's mind and makes as if to pronounce 'car', then the retraction of the tongue on the soft palate is at once perceptible. This does not entail problems for the pronunciation of Arabic, in which similar front-to-back variation occurs as between e.g. kiis 'sack; purse' and kuuz 'clay jug'.

As in the case of t (see p. 42), k is often slightly aspirated, but the aspiration associated with the corresponding English sound is quite unacceptable and the learner should aim at a completely unaspirated plosive, with a following vowel beginning immediately on release of the stop. Unaspirated k occurs in English, for example in the initial cluster sk- of 'skin', 'scoop', etc., and the isolation of the sound from this context will help. If one imagines one is going to say 'skin' but says instead 'kin', then an unaspirated initial plosive should result. Similarly, an unaspirated k in 'coop' may be learned from imagining it preceded by the s of 'scoop'. It is an easy matter thereafter to use an unaspirated k in Arabic examples like káyfa 'how', káafir 'unbeliever', ka9k 'cakes', etc. Reduced aspiration is characteristic of some regional dialects of English, for instance in parts of Yorkshire and in Scottish English.

One further noteworthy feature is that k is released *audibly* before t in e.g. yáktub 'he writes', which contrasts markedly with the inaudible release of English k in e.g. 'actor'.

Further examples of k: kaan 'he was', kúufii 'Kufic (writing)', makáan 'place', sakt 'silence', mask 'seizure, detention', śukúuk 'doubts'.

q: A voiceless uvular plosive, which occurs in other Asian languages, e.g. Urdu. To pronounce q properly is not simply to make k as far back as possible, as instructions often have it. More is involved than just raising the back of the tongue to the uvula. It was earlier said that the root and epiglottal parts of the tongue fill the throat, that the tonsillar arches are contracted inwards, and that the trachea rises. These are connected movements, and, although in the nature of things the first two are not open to normal inspection, nevertheless the third may be indirectly observed by watching the Adam's apple and the external throat area above it, which rise as the trachea rises. Repeating a series of q sounds, making and breaking contact between tongue and uvula at rapid, regular intervals, resembles the pouring of liquid from a narrow-necked bottle, and the accompanying up-and-down movement of the Adam's apple and associated area is immediately evident. The sound is quite unlike k, although it is similarly subject to fronting and backing in response to vowel context. It is important for Arabic learning to develop a feel for the uvular region, indeed for the whole region of the throat. For those comparatively few English speakers from the north-east of England who use a uvular r, and for those who successfully imitate the uvular r of northern and south-western French, it is easy to feel the region in which the closure for q must be made. It is then just a matter of closing off the friction for this variety of r at the place where it is made. The mirror can be a useful aid when learning q.

Practising q in different vowel environments is essential. Although the amount of movement from u to q is small, it is likely that acquisition of the sound will follow more readily from a starting-point of as far back an *open* vowel as possible, from the sound one makes when invited to say 'ah' with the doctor's spatula down the throat. From this position, movement of the extreme back of the tongue to the uvula is minimal. The uvula is considerably lower than the rest of the palate, and it is, therefore, not surprising that q has a noticeable opening influence on adjoining vowels. This is especially so in the case of close front vowels, which are marked not only by centralization in juxtaposition with q but also by a central vocalic glide on to the consonant, as in riiq [riː°q][1] 'saliva, spittle'. On- and off-glides are an important diagnostic feature of most sounds, not least stops, and those relating to k and q are as different as the overall sound complexes involved. Off-glides at once reveal the nature of the preceding consonant, and the central-to-open glide from final q in e.g. b@qq 'bugs' stands in striking contrast with the much fronter and closer glide that characterizes the release of (k)k in šakk 'doubt'.

It is worth any trouble to acquire a good pronunciation of q,

---

[1] The diaeresis indicates a centralized quality of the vowel above which it appears.

which is so often a sign of the prestigious literary and Classical language. Apart from certain lexical items, e.g. q@ryah 'village', q is usually replaced by ? in vernacular Egyptian Arabic of an urban kind and has a reflex g in some rural dialects, much less often k. The relationship between q and ? is a subtle one in educated Cairene speech, but it will not detain us, since, for present purposes, q alone is required. In other regions, variation involving q and j occurs, and in Kuwait and Iraq, for instance, the intricate relations in vernacular Arabic between q, g, j, and even y are of considerable interest, with variants determined lexically or phonologically and often occurring within the same root. Again, in certain dialectal forms of Palestinian and Jordanian Arabic, q has been either considerably fronted or replaced by k, and among educated Palestinians in particular the voiceless uvular plosive (q) is often stigmatized as a mark of rustic speech and replaced in conversation by ?. Intrinsically interesting as such matters are, they are not relevant to the Classical Arabic and reading style of our concern, within which q is the norm. ?, for its part, is the sound of hámzah, not a reflex of q, whereas g is an occasional variant of j.

q, again surprisingly, since it is a voiceless sound like T earlier, is one of ?alħurúufu lmuq@lq@lah, with a central vocalic off-glide to silence in Quranic recitation, though again this is not strictly our business. In some rural dialects, and more regularly in bedouin speech, to which exegetists have often turned, a voiced velar plosive g does occur as the counterpart of q elsewhere.

Examples of q: q@@l 'he said', qíimah 'value, worth', qúllah 'top, summit', T@ríiq@h 'manner, means', miqyáas 'measure, measurement; gauge', b@rq 'lightning; telegraph', T@ríiq 'way, road'.

(v) GUTTURALS

(a) uvular fricatives (x, ğ)

x ğ: Having acquired q, the learner should find little difficulty in learning the uvular fricatives. The stop should be released sufficiently to allow fricative passage of air, with enough breath force to ensure the characteristic 'rasp' or 'scrape' of x. For ğ, the same buzz of voice is introduced into x as that for z from the starting-point of s. Alternatively, since the articulation of ğ is also that of uvular r, those who can pronounce the latter need simply to unvoice it for x. If there are still problems of acquisition, the sounds may be learned from others of a familiar but non-linguistic kind. Thus, x (and the vibration attached to it) can be equated with breathing out heavily during snoring. The inspirational vibration felt during this activity is indeed of the soft palate and the return expiration should do satisfactorily for x. If ġ, for its part, is not learned from x in accordance with the earlier instructions, then it can readily be acquired from 'dry gargling', since we rarely succeed when gargling in reaching parts beyond the uvula.

Examples of x: x@fíif 'light' (s.m.), xiSb 'facility, abundance', xurm 'hole', n@xr 'snoring; snorting', f@rx@h 'young hen-bird', tafríix 'hatching; incubation', mun@@x (or man@@x) 'climate'.

Examples of ġ: ġ@fíir 'watchman; guard', ġiT@@? 'cover', y@ġúTT 'he immerses', b@ġ@@ 'he wished for', śuġl 'work', r@ġma 'in spite of', ?alġ@@m '(explosive) mines', r@ww@@ġ 'cunning, crafty', taswíiġ 'leasing (out)'.

(b) *pharyngal fricatives* (ħ 9)

ħ 9: These pharyngal fricatives, voiceless and voiced, though they do occur in some other languages, are particularly associated with Arabic, and provide good further examples of how non-linguistic activities in the mechanism of utterance can be turned to good account in learning pronunciation. In brief, during the articulation of these pharyngal sounds, the epiglottis and the root of the tongue fuse together and are drawn back and down to narrow the air-passage between them and the pharynx wall, while the trachea and larynx rise, thus reducing the gap between the trachea and the under-surface of the epiglottal fold. Looking inside the mouth in a mirror reveals some reflex raising of the uvular region of the soft palate but no movement of the visible parts of the tongue, which should be kept flat on the floor of the mouth. To master the sounds, it is necessary to 'get the feel' of the throat region above the trachea or windpipe. By placing the finger on the Adam's apple one can see and feel what happens to the larynx in swallowing. It clearly rises considerably then descends again to its position of rest. It is helpful to concentrate on this larynx movement, and to keep the larynx at the top of its run instead of allowing it to descend—the discomfort felt will be in the region where it is necessary to make ħ and 9. Upward movement of the larynx is essential for the production of these consonants, though the excursion is not as great as in swallowing. The reason for this is that in swallowing, and also in retching, the top of the trachea is seated on the under-surface of the epiglottal fold, so that nothing may 'go down the wrong way' into the bronchial tubes and lungs. Alternate raising and lowering of the larynx from rest involves tightening and relaxing of the throat muscles, but, from a practical point of view, the best way of stimulating the relevant musculature and of familiarizing oneself with the organs involved is to adopt a retching posture prior to releasing the tension in the pharynx just enough to allow egress of air—the result should be an acceptable ħ. Other ways of developing a feel for the pharyngal region include the rasping or scraping of the pharynx wall, sometimes heard prior to expectoration, and even the trilling of the epiglottis. Again, sufficient relaxation of the rasp or trill will produce ħ. It is possible, too, to produce a pharyngal stop,[1] which may well be made when adopting the retching posture. From the stop position, it is again an easy matter to release the stop just enough to give the desired pharyngal fricative sound, with the throat filled by the extreme back of the tongue above the windpipe. The pharyngal fricatives will almost certainly not be learned over-night, and much practice and experimentation is usually needed. The learner often passes through early stages of unwanted sound— for instance, by positioning the tongue parallel to the pharynx wall, he often produces a sound which combines features of ħ and x. Again, forcing air through the glottis or through space in the cartilaginous material at the rear of the vocal cords in what has been termed 'stage whisper' produces sounds which, though unusual, are unacceptable as pharyngal fricatives. It also has to be said that ħ is not in the least like either x or h and must always be clearly distinguished from them.

As ġ is to x, or z to s, so 9 is to ħ, i.e. its voiced correlative. From the starting-point of ħ, it is important to do no more than introduce the buzz of voice for 9. It is true that in much of Syria, Kuwait, and Iraq, 9 is usually glottalized, i.e. pronounced with a simultaneous glottal stop, but in Egypt, North Africa, and much of the Levant, 9 is simply the voiced counterpart of ħ. It is possible, and good practice, to imbue speech with the sound of 9 throughout. The effect is of 'strangled', 'growl-like' sound, but it should not be thought, as it sometimes has been thought, that a feature of 9 is what is known to phoneticians as 'creaky voice', so no attention should

---

[1] A sound which occurs, as a variant of q, in the Arabic of Fez in Morocco, as in məqli 'fried'.

be paid by the learner to suggestions that have been made to 'sing down to your bottom note—and then one lower'. It is perfectly possible to sing a scale on 9, though it is noteworthy that there is a marked fall in pitch and volume when 9 follows, say, a vowel, and a corresponding rise in pitch and volume when a vowel follows. The 'strangled' effect is also more or less marked according to region. The impression of strong or weak articulation derives from the degree of pharyngal narrowing, of larynx raising, and generally of muscular tension. Egyptian pronunciation, Classical or vernacular, is characterized by the strong articulation of 9, in contrast, for example, with typical Syrian practice.

Once control of the processes of pharyngalization has been achieved, it becomes important to 'turn it on and off' at the right time in the stream of speech. It was said above that it is possible to pharyngalize the whole of speech, and a common early error is to impart pharyngal quality to a preceding vowel, which is offensive to an Arab ear. The same fault may occur in relation to following vowels, but is more easily eradicated. Practice is therefore important between vowels, both short and long, i.e. a(a)–9-a(a), a(a)-9-i(i), a(a)-9-u(u), i(i)-9-a(a), i(i)-9-i(i), i(i)-9-u(u), u(u)-9-a(a), u(u)-9-i(i), u(u)-9-u(u), a-99-aa, a-99-ii, a-99-uu, a-99-a, i-99-i, u-99-u, etc. To ensure that pharyngal quality is not imparted to adjoining vowels, to the first vowel, for example, of fágala 'he did' or nágam 'yes', it is helpful at first to split the form into its constituent syllables, i.e. fa-ga-la, na-gam, before running them together as in normal pronunciation. Practice, too, will be needed of both ḥ and 9 in pre- and post-consonantal occurrence, e.g. baḥt 'research', r@9d 'thunder', sábḥah '(a) swim', qíT9ah 'piece, morsel', milḥ 'salt', f@r9 'branch'. Vowel-glides on to and off from ḥ and 9 are even more noticeable, and more noticeably open in quality, than in the case of q, e.g. riiḥ [rïː^ḥ][1] 'wind', qíT9ah [qït^ɑʕah][2] 'piece'. If articulation is correctly performed, the glide in a given example will, so to speak, 'make itself'. Special practice will probably be necessary in the case of examples in which the pharyngals and the close front vowel are in juxtaposition, whether the fricative follows, as in riiḥ, or precedes, as in 9íisaa 'Jesus'.

Finally, differentiation practice is particularly valuable between

---

[1] ʌ symbolizes a vowel that typically occurs in the southern standard English pronunciation of 'but'.

[2] [ʕ] is the IPA symbol for a voiced pharyngal fricative (9).

ħ, h, and x, and between 9, ?, and ǧ. Illustrative contrasts are: ħammáam 'bath'/hammáam 'worried'/x@mmáas 'sharecropper', ħíilah 'ruse, trick'/híinah 'facility; ease'/xíir@h 'the best', s@ħr 'lungs'/sahl 'easy' (s.m.)/s@xf 'feeble-mindedness', salħ 'excrement'/k@rh 'hatred'/salx 'skinning', 9állab 'he canned, preserved'/ ?állaf 'he accustomed; tamed'/ǧ@llab 'he made s.o. triumph', ságal(a) 'he coughed'/sá?al(a) 'he asked'/ś@ǧ@l(a) 'he kept s.o. busy', t@Sníi9 'industrialization'/malíi? 'replete'/tafríiǧ 'emptying'.

Further examples of ħ: ħámal 'he carried; he lifted', ħáajah 'need', ħuur 'houris', ħumúulah '(load) capacity', ħiinámaa 'while, when', r@ħal 'he set out', muħíiT 'circumference; ocean', ríħlah 'journey', Súlħii 'peacemaking, arbitrational', mus@TT@ħ 'flat, even', t@Slíiħ 'restoration, repair', ruuħ 'soul, spirit', Subħ 'daybreak; morning'.

Further examples of 9: 9ámal 'work; activity', 9índa 'at, by, with', 9iid 'feast, festival', 9uud 'stick, pole', 9únuq 'neck, nape of neck', ma9áamil 'factories', maa9úun 'utensil', lá9nah 'curse', sáb9ah 'seven', mur@bba9 'fourfold; quadrangular', r@bíi9 '(season of) spring', ?usbúu9 'week', rub9 'quarter'.

(c) glottal fricative and plosive (h; ?)

h: The symbol for breath or voicelessness, and, indeed, during the sound it symbolizes, the glottis is typically wide open. The sound, often if somewhat unhappily termed 'fricative' as part of the label 'glottal fricative', may have the resonance of any vowel in response to the shape adopted by the supra-glottal resonating cavities. It is, of course, the usual English sound occurring initially in 'hat' or 'hard', but there are English speakers who produce weak velar or uvular friction for h by raising the back of the tongue too close to the soft palate. Needless to say, this should be avoided, since Arabic h is always clearly distinguished from x. For the great majority of English speakers, however, h will pose no problems when it is initial in a word or syllable, as in híya 'she', hawáa? 'air', or muhímm 'important'. Difficulty will arise when the sound closes a syllable or is one of two consonants closing a syllable, as in mahbúul 'stupid', bih 'with him', kitáabah[1] 'writing', duhn 'oil',

---

[1] -h of the feminine singular and unit-ending is pronounced in a 'strict Classical' accent. It is usually omitted in 'ordinary conversation', which is not, of course, our concern.

and k@rh 'hatred'. These are un-English contexts for h and the tendency of the English speaker will be to make h sound like x. It can help to insert an extra 'ghost' vowel following h in e.g. *mahabúul etc. and to eliminate it gradually. Having dealt satisfactorily in this way with the first h of, say, q@hwah 'coffee; café', the same device may be used for final h, i.e. from the starting-point of *q@hwaha.

If more breath force is used than is necessary simply to make the vocal cords vibrate for voice, then both voice and friction occur at the glottis for what is known as 'voiced h'. Intervocalic h is often of this kind in English 'behind', etc. and also occurs in Arabic, perhaps especially before a voiced consonant as in mahbuul [mafi-];[1] cf. ?áhtam 'toothless' (s.m.), in which the glottis is more likely to be wide open for h. In some cases, the occurrence of 'voiced h' is optional, as in duhn 'oil', variously [-fin] or [-hn̥], and, when final, the sound often combines the two types, e.g. kitaabah [-fiᵇ], with a 'breathy' or voiceless off-glide to pause. All consonants are to be pronounced in Arabic—final h, occurring as it does in e.g. k@rh in a way to which English speakers are unaccustomed, cannot be omitted. Finally, following a vowel, final h is usually of the 'voiced' variety, and, to avoid pronouncing it like x, use may be made of the earlier stratagem of first including before eliminating a final 'ghost' vowel in e.g. *taahᵃ 'he lost his way', *tiihⁱ 'wilderness; maze'.

Other examples of h: háadi? 'calm', muttáhim 'accuser', z@hr@h 'blossom', burháan 'proof', mub@@r@@h 'contest, match'.

?: The glottal stop or catch, produced by closing the vocal cords, as we do when we fix the diaphragm prior to lifting a heavy weight, then suddenly separating them. By definition, the sound is neither voiced nor voiceless, since it is not physically possible to combine either feature with plosion at the vocal cords.

The sound is common enough in English. It occurs, for example, between words beginning and ending with a vowel, e.g. 'Jaffa ?orange', and also when it is wished to give special prominence to a word beginning with a vowel, e.g. 'It's ?absolutely ?awful'. It is a feature of a number of English dialects, where it often corresponds to orthographic t, as in Cockney and Glaswegian pronunciation of

---

[1] [fi] is the IPA symbol for 'voiced h'.

'bottle', 'a bit o' butter', etc. In London and the north-east of England, it will be heard following voiceless stops, as in 'copper' [-p?-].[1] Students of German will be familiar with it preceding any vowel-beginning word, e.g. ?in ?einem ?alten Buch 'in an old book'. In Arabic there are two roles played by the glottal stop. In the first place, it may be a radical of a given root like any other, e.g. báda? 'he began', and in the second, it may be used to obviate vowel-beginning utterance, which is unacceptable in the Classical form of the language. These two functions are labelled respectively hamzátu lq@T9 'the hámzah (= glottal stop) of cutting', where the reference is to the cutting off of voice by the abrupt coming together of the vocal cords, and hamzátu lw@Sl 'the hámzah of joining', which refers to the use of a glottal stop post-pausally, followed by a supporting vowel, the latter serving to obviate a cluster-beginning form and the glottal stop in turn obviating a vowel-beginning form. An example of hamzátu lw@Sl is the term itself. The isolate form ?alw@Sl, where ? prevents vowel-beginning and -a- prevents a sequence of three consonants, appears as lw@Sl in conjunction with preceding hamzátu, i.e. with both ?- and -a- omitted. We return to hamzátu lw@Sl in detail in 6.2.

Problems of pronunciation are likely to arise, as with h, when ? occurs pre-consonantally, e.g. r@?s 'head', and finally, e.g. zánna? 'he restricted', bad? 'beginning', but also importantly when ? is post-consonantal and pre-vocalic, e.g. the second ? of ?al?áan 'now'. The presence of this ? is in marked contrast with its absence in ?aláan 'he softened; he soothed'. It is of great importance that, wherever ? occurs, the voice should be cut off completely, in this case after l. When we 'hold our breath', the vocal cords come together as for the glottal stop. The fact may be made use of, if difficulty is found with e.g. ?al?áan, by pausing slightly after l and in similar places elsewhere. As generally with contrasting sounds, it may be necessary to train oneself to *hear* as well as to make the contrast in question. In the case of ?, concentration on the cutting off of the voice should be helpful.

Noticeably less use of ? is made in vernacular than in Classical Arabic. In the bedouin dialect of Cyrenaica in Libya, for example, the sound does not occur at all, whereas in Egypt it is more often a reflex of q, though it does occur with other interpretations. It is not

---

[1] [?] is the IPA symbol for the glottal stop.

surprising, however, to find that in Egyptian vernacular Arabic r@@s 'head', ruus 'heads' correspond to Classical r@?s and ru?úus. ?, with w and y, is a 'weak' radical even in the Classical language, and is subject to elision and mutation under certain circumstances. In Egyptian speech, one finds alongside the educated form r@?íis 'chief, head' and its plural form rú?asa (CA ru?asáa?) the etymologically related r@yyis/rúyasa 'ganger(s)', and the example could be greatly multiplied. There is a tendency, too, for initial ? to be pronounced rather more weakly than in other positions, more particularly in the Levant and especially in Syro-Lebanese speech. Classical ? is often subject to 'modification', especially when first radical of a root. Thus, it is omitted in the imperative of some verbs, e.g. xud 'take!' (s.m.) (cf. ?@x@d 'he t̊ook') and is replaced by u in others, e.g. ?úumul (not *?u?mul) 'hope!' (s.m.). These forms arise from the unacceptability of two successive glottal stops, and for the same reason ?aa- replaces *?a?- in the 1st person singular non-past or imperfect tense, e.g. ?áalaf (for *?a?laf) 'I am familiar with', and ?ii- replaces *?i?- in the verbal form VIII, e.g. ?iitálaf (for *?i?talaf) 'he was closely connected with'. It should be noted, however, that these forms with long vowel are post-pausal, and that in juncture the original radical ? remains, as in fá ?mul 'so hope!', wa ?tálaf 'and he was connected with'.

Further examples of ?: ?asáas 'foundation', ?át@r 'trace, vestige', ?ibn[1] 'son', ?úmmah 'nation', r@?aa 'he saw', masáa?il 'problems', ?as?ílah 'questions', yáb?us 'he is miserable', śa?n 'matter, affair', bi?r 'well', juz? 'part; fraction', ?alm@r? 'man, human being; one', śur@káa? 'partners', baadíi? 'beginning, outset', m@qrúu? 'read, recited'.

(VI) SEMIVOWELS (w, y)

w: A labio-velar semivowel like English w in 'woo', which it closely resembles when initial in the word or syllable, e.g. wájad 'he found', dawáah 'ink-well', śákwah 'complaint', but even in these contexts Arabic w is pronounced more vigorously than its English counterpart, and care also needs to be taken over the rounding and protrusion of the lips. The consonantal nature of w betokened by these features is even more in evidence in Egyptian Classical pronunciation when it occurs pre-consonantally (always following

---

[1] An example of hamzátu lw@śl.

the open vowel), e.g. ṭawb 'garment', lawḥ 'board', káwkab 'star', and especially in final position, both post-vocalic and post-consonantal, e.g. law 'if', f@rw 'furs', filw 'foal', 9uDw 'member, limb'. Final and post-consonantal, w may occur voiceless, especially after a voiceless consonant, e.g. 9afw̥ 'forgiveness'.

Pre-consonantal -aw- has often been described as diphthongal, but this is misleading when the closest possible lip-rounding and tongue-raising together with considerable muscular tension in both tongue and lips characterize the sound of w in strict Classical pronunciation. It is only in certain forms of vernacular Arabic that -aw- is realized phonetically as a diphthong of an approximately half-open to half-close type [ʌo], and, indeed, Classical -aw- usually corresponds in the vernacular Arabic of Egypt and elsewhere to a mid back rounded monophthong or pure vowel [ǫ].[1] In very relaxed style, diphthongization and even monophthongization may occur in Classical pronunciation but are better avoided. The afore-mentioned tense features of w should be aimed at in all contexts, but are probably most noticeable when the consonant is final, or is geminated, or follows the close back rounded vowel uu, e.g. dáww@r 'he turned, he rotated', 9adúuw[2] 'enemy' (s.m.), 9adúuwah 'enemy' (s.f.).

y: A palatal semivowel similar to English y in 'yield', but concerning which qualifications must be made similar to those applied above to w. The English example 'woo' was deliberately chosen under w, since w is more closely rounded before the close back vowel represented by '-oo' in the spelling than before, say, '-e-' in 'wet', and this close rounding is characteristic of Arabic w in all contexts in CARS. Similarly, y in English 'yield' is closer as to tongue position and more spread as to lip position than y in e.g. 'yet'. Once again, it is the English y of 'yield' that provides the closer parallel to Arabic y. Although 'semivowel' is a reasonable description of y when it occurs initially in word or syllable, e.g. yáabis 'dry, dried up', máryam 'Mary', ṭaaníyan 'secondly', tasmíyah 'naming', nevertheless the space between front of tongue and hard palate is very small, lip-spreading is vigorous, and muscular tension in tongue and lips is again marked. As in the case of w, special notice should be taken of y when it occurs pre-

---

[1] The hook denotes an open variety of the vowel indicated.
[2] Which could as well be transcribed 9adúww.

consonantally following the open vowel, e.g. S@yf 'summer', báyna 'between', and also finally, post-vocalic and post-consonantal, where the muscular tension spoken of is particularly noticeable, e.g. ?ay 'that is, i.e.', tady 'breast, udder', 9umy 'blind' (pl.). The consonantal nature of the sound appears clearly in its optional rendering in 9umy as a partially voiceless, palatal fricative. Like -aw-, pre-consonantal -ay- often corresponds to a diphthong [ɛɪ] in vernacular Arabic, and again, in the vernacular speech of Egypt, its reflex is a mid front spread monophthong [ɛ].[1] Concerned, however, as we are with Classical pronunciation, this need not detain us, though these pronunciations may be heard in very relaxed style. Yet again, the aforementioned consonantal features, especially those of muscular tension and palatal friction, are most in evidence when y is geminated or follows the close front spread vowel ii, e.g. láyyan 'he softened', kayy ($\sqrt{}$kwy) 'burning, cauterization' (contrast ?ay), riyy (or r@yy) ($\sqrt{}$rwy) 'quenching thirst; irrigating', mansíiy 'forgotten', yawmíiyah 'daily wage' (contrast e.g. tasmíyah 'naming'), fal@sTiiniiyíin 'Palestinians'.[2]

w and y are both weak radicals and have much in common in addition to phonetic behaviour. For example, each may replace the other in a given paradigm, as in the case of tiyáab 'clothes', plural of tawb 'garment'. Elsewhere, choice may obtain between them, as when both lahw and lahy occur in the sense of 'insult(ing)'. Other similarities might be adduced, but those mentioned suffice to underline further the parallelism of behaviour between the two semivowels.

4.2 Gemination of consonants (tašdíid)[3]

Gemination or doubling of consonants is an important device of Arabic morphology, and any consonant may be doubled intervocalically and finally. Though there occurs sometimes, under vernacular influence, a reduction of length in final position, this should be resisted and a geminated consonant pronounced at least twice as

---

[1] An open variety of [e].

[2] No distinction of pronunciation would correspond to variant spellings -iiy-/iyy- and -iiy-/-iyy-.

[3] tašdíid 'strengthening, intensifying' is the feature or process of gemination, šáddah its written sign, and a given geminated consonant is referred to as mušad-dádah (feminine, since the letters of the alphabet are usually treated as feminine).

long as its single counterpart. Geminated consonants are also characterized by greater muscular tension in the articulating organs. Any lengthening of consonants in English is on a totally different basis from Arabic and is comparatively infrequent. It occurs at the junction of words, e.g. 'mad dog', 'wall-light', 'black king', 'up-platform', and also at that of affixes and words, e.g. 'unnecessary', 'midday', 'misshapen'. Some people distinguish 'wholly' from 'holy' by doubling l in the former, but this is optional in English, whereas gemination is always obligatory in Arabic. It is, therefore, not only the actual realization of gemination that many English speakers find difficult in certain contexts (to be specified below) but also the need to remember to geminate at the right places, which involves acquiring new habits running counter to English ones. English spelling, it need hardly be said, with its phonetically ungeminated -tt- of 'butter' or -ll of 'bell', etc., is of no help whatever.

English speakers find it comparatively easy to geminate consonants when the second member of the geminate pair initiates the accented syllable, as in ?@ll@@h 'Allah, God', dukkáan, 'shop', majjáanan 'free, gratis', yaśummúunah 'they smell it (m.)', kallámat 'she spoke to s.o.'. Elsewhere, the incidence of the accent leads to difficulties of two opposing kinds—mistakenly lengthening non-geminated consonants, on the one hand, and, on the other, failing to give geminated consonants their due length and consequent weight in the quantitative rhythmic patterns of forms. Gemination is facilitated in ?@ll@@h by its immediately pre-accentual position, but in e.g. naśśaalúun 'thieves, pickpockets' it occurs at some remove from the accent and the intervening long vowel constitutes an additional difficulty, since the pattern CVC (naś-) CVV (-śaa-) CV́VC (-lúun) is foreign to English, and indeed to Egyptian vernacular Arabic, in which long vowels do not occur in unaccented syllables. The tendency of the English learner, faced by the need to observe the length of both consonant and vowel, will be to reduce the first two syllables of naśśaalúun to the type CV. He should remember that the CA syllable must always begin with a consonant and that, whenever gemination occurs, it must be seen to comprise two consonants of which the first closes and the second opens a syllable, with or without any new breath-impulse between them. Aiming at making a new breath-impulse 'half-way through' śś in naśśaalúun should produce the desired result, if at the same time the length of the vowel in the -śaa- syllable is respected. In the case of plosives, it is, of course, the stop phase that must be maintained for an appreciable time, as in b@TT@@lúun 'inactive' (pl.). It is better to pronounce a geminate consonant extremely long than not long enough. Other examples for practice are qubbatáan 'two domes', m@rr@táyn 'twice', ʔaśśitáa? 'the winter', sayy@@r@tuhu 'his car', kallamtúhaa 'I spoke to her', ʔittif@@qiiyáat 'agreements', yataɣallamúun 'they learn', li ruk-kaabíhaa 'for its (f.) passengers'.

The opposing error of unwantedly lengthening non-geminated consonants again derives from accentual incidence, and again, the realization of forms in terms of their constituent syllables provides the answer to any difficulty encountered. The t, s, and l of e.g. kátabah 'clerks', kás@r 'he broke', and kálimah 'word' are often undesirably lengthened following the short accented vowel, and to overcome this, forms should be split into syllables, i.e. ká-ta-bah, ká-s@r, ká-li-mah, which should then be gradually run together. An English tendency, therefore, is to pronounce -s- in kás@r too long and -ss- in káss@r 'he smashed' too short, whereas in Arabic the non-geminated and geminated counterparts are always clearly differentiated, as again between, say, b@T@l 'hero' and b@TT@l 'he neutralized, nullified'. The accented syllable is initial in the foregoing examples, but this need not be so, and the same difficulty may arise with, say, ʔaħadúhumaa 'each one of the two', in which -h- must not be prolonged, even in the absence of any geminate contrast. Other examples of gemination immediately following the accent are dálluu 'they showed', mufáttiś 'inspector', ʔuurúbbaa 'Europe', and there are many others.

Final gemination may pose a problem. In Egyptian vernacular Arabic, shortening in this context is quite frequent, though the muscular tension spoken of earlier is always present in contrast with final non-geminates. Moreover, a final -CV(V)CC syllable is always accented. In any case, in the Classical language, the length of all final geminates must be maintained, even of voiceless stops, as in sitt 'six', ś@TT 'shore, coast', b@qq 'bugs', in which the stop is released audibly. An example of final non-geminate/geminate contrast is sal (more often, ʔís?al) 'ask!' (s.m.)/dall 'he showed'. Polysyllables with final gemination need cause no difficulty, e.g. yadúll 'he shows', except probably when the geminate is preceded by a long vowel, as in mawáadd 'products, materials' (contrast

?iijáad 'obtaining') or ʒaamm 'public, general' (contrast ʒaam 'year').

Here, finally, are a few further examples for practice: ?aśśáddah 'the śáddah' (the written sign of taśdíid 'gemination'), ?attilmíid 'the pupil', ?assamáa? 'the sky', r@@m@ll@(h) 'Ramalla' (Palestinian town), ?ittiħáad 'unity', sayasurrúnii 'it will please me, I shall be pleased', yuħadditáan 'they (two) tell, relate', ħaajj 'pilgrim'. The following illustrate further the contrast between non-geminate and geminate: fátaħ 'he opened'/fáttaħ 'he caused to open', hawáa? 'air'/hawwáa? 'amateur'/háwwaa 'he ventilated', tan@@Ð@r 'he faced s.o.'/tan@ÐÐ@r 'he watched closely', t@r@k 'he left'/mifákk 'screwdriver', ʒáamil 'worker'/ʒummáal 'workers', ʒawwáam '(good) swimmer'/ʒawáamm 'populace'.

5

THE ARABIC VOWELS

5.1 General

The greatly different nature of the English and Arabic vowel systems has already been briefly spoken of (pp. 18–19). The first division that requires to be made for Arabic is a twofold one between vowel and zero in the processes of syllable patterning. The Arabic (consonant-)letter has the inherent implication C±V, where −V = zero-vowel. The positive term (+V) is in Arabic ḥ@r@kah 'movement; vowel', with the threefold subdivision of fátḥah (a/@), kásr@h (i), and D@mmah (u); zero-vowel is termed in Arabic sukúun 'rest; vowellessness'.[1] The terminology invokes the metaphor of the free flow or movement of speech in the form of open syllables (CV) and its arrest by the application of sukúun to a consonant, which then directly precedes another (CC). A letter is said to be mutaḥ@rríkah[2] 'moved or moving; vowelled', and, if so, variously maftúuḥah (Ca), maksúur@h (Ci), and m@Dmúumah (Cu), as opposed to saakínah or musakkánah 'resting; vowelless'. Thus, sukúun and ḥ@r@kah are used to distinguish, for example, monosyllabic f@rš 'spreading; furniture' from disyllabic f@r@š 'he spread out', in which r is variously saakínah (or musakkánah) and mutaḥ@rríkah (specifically, maftúuḥah).

Concern in this chapter will be with the three positive vowel-units or ḥ@r@káat. Though the vocalic qualities associated with them greatly exceed three, in response mainly to consonantal context, nevertheless systematic differentiation is never more than three-fold. This regular distinction of three vowel phonemes is typical of Classical Arabic and does not always apply to the spoken language, in which certain vernaculars distinguish for the most part only two short vowels, others again four, and distinctions between short and long vowels, in contrast with CA, are rarely congruent. At the sonant level, too, it is a widespread feature of vernacular Arabic

---

[1] The term also applies, of course, to the written sign of vowellessness.
[2] The letters of the alphabet are more often than not treated as feminine.

that close vowels are subject to elision in contexts where open vowels are not. In the matter of vowel differences, then, Classical Arabic is *sui generis* and the vowels are not so much a means of ensuring intelligibility as of indicating the speaker's prowess as an Arabic grammarian. The apparently limited repertoire of vowel discriminations should not, however, be taken to mean that Arabic suffers from a paucity of differential devices. On the contrary, by ringing the changes between roots and also within (and without) roots by means of several types of affixation, vowel differentiation, the length feature, gemination, and the like, the patterning potential of Arabic becomes almost limitless.

The ancient Arab grammarians were excellent phoneticians and their choice of vowel terminology is indicative of their general phonetic awareness. The term fátḥah 'opening' designates the vowel sign which indicates the feature of openness (fatḥ); kásr@h 'breaking, cracking' refers to the diacritic which in turn indicates spreading of the lips (kasr) in contrast with the reference of D@mmah 'gathering together' to the sign for labial rounding and protrusion (D@mm). It is necessary, of course, to add the dimension of tongue-raising and to distinguish between front raising for kásr@h (a close front spread vowel) and back raising for D@mmah (a close back rounded vowel). Frontness or backness in relation to fátḥah is not specified and it will be seen in 5.3 that variation in open vowel quality is a function of the consonant context. The choice has nevertheless been made in this book of a transcriptional distinction between front a and back @ as a practical 'aid to reading' for English speakers, for whom the difference of vowel between, say, 'cam' and 'calm' is considerable. At the same time it must be understood that this further 'aid to reading' does not betoken an addition to the Classical Arabic system of three vowel phonemes and that it is perfectly possible to design rules by which the proper pronunciation may be assigned to any given occurrence of the vowel-unit fátḥah. This would not be feasible, however, for e.g. Egyptian vernacular Arabic, in which the difference between front and back varieties of open vowel is often unpredictable. Whereas a triangular diagram would satisfy the facts of the Classical language, a quadrilateral figure

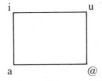

is better adapted to those of its spoken Egyptian counterpart.

5.2 The length feature

On a par with gemination as a syllabic quantitative and morphological device is the lengthening (madd) of the three vowels, each of which is subject to a short/long contrast (a/aa (@/@@), i/ii, u/uu). Syllable types are reducible to three quantities—short (CV), medium (CVV, CVC), and long (CVVC, CVCC, CVVCC)—and the types CVV, CVVC, and CVVCC are differentiated quantitatively from CV, CVC, and CVCC by incremental vowel length, indicated in the script by the 'letters of prolongation' (ḥurúufu lmádd, i.e. ?álif (aa, @@), waaw (uu), and yaa? (ii) (?al?álifu/?alwáawu/?alyáa?u llayyínah)). The doubled letter has been used in this book to mark vowel length and serves to underline both the parallelism between it and consonantal gemination and the correspondence between long vowels and their more abstract symbolization as VV. The indication of vowel length is the sole concession in regard to vowelling which is made to the reader in the body of the Arabic script. The superscript sign máddah, adapted from a horizontal ?álif, should perhaps be mentioned. It is only used with ?álif and, in word-initial position, has the phonetic value ?aa-. Medially, saa?ála 'he interrogated s.o.' and qir@@?ah 'reading' are, or, perhaps better, have been, sometimes spelt with máddah, though ?álif followed by hámzah is the usual practice nowadays. As far as uu and ii are concerned, when recourse was had to indicating long vowels in the script, the phonetic similarity was recognized between consonantal w/y and the close back and front vowels u/i, and so thereafter the symbols for w and y were used as 'aids to reading' in the Arabic writing of uu and ii.

Before a following vowel or pause, little or no phonetic distinction seems to be made between -iiy(V/‡) and -iyy, -uuw(V/‡) and

-uww. Any difference between, let us say, 9adúuw 'enemy' (√9dw) and *9adúww, níiyah 'intention; will' (√nwy) and *níyyah, would appear to be hypothetical, though the first forms are to be preferred in the absence of any morphological motivation for the forms with gemination. There would, however, often be no reason against writing—in an Arabic way—iy instead of ii, when a consonant follows or the relevant syllable is final and unaccented, e.g. *r@Díyt 'you (s.m.) were pleased' as opposed to r@Díit (√rDy), *y@rmiy 'he throws' as opposed to y@rmii (√rmy). In some cases it is important to distinguish between short i followed by the semivowel y, used as a syllable-divider between vowels,[1] e.g. tatníyah (verbal noun) 'seconding, supporting', and long ii also followed by intervocalic y, e.g. mansíiyah (s.f. passive participle) 'forgotten' (√nsy). The transcription *mansíyyah would suggest more immediately the high degree of muscular tension used in pronunciation, but morphology again favours mansíiyah. The so-called 'relative' (nísbah) termination -iiy is treated similarly, though in the script y may appear with sáddah, the mark also of gemination. There is fluctuation among lexicographers and grammarians in the way this termination is written in roman form—one sees, for example, muusawii 'Mosaic' (law, etc.), samaawii 'heavenly', etc., but the Classical accentuation muusawíiy (with final muscular tension and palatal friction), samaawíiy, etc., indicates that the ultimate syllable must be long (-CVVC), not medium (-CVV). In the vernacular language this syllable is not treated as long and accentuation is associated with the penultimate syllable in such forms as ?ingilíizi (CA ?ingiliizíiy) 'English', fal@sTíini (CA fal@sTiiníiy) 'Palestinian', etc. The occurrence of -uw-, short u+pre-vocalic semivowel w, is rare. It appears in the past tense of some 'stative' verbs, e.g. T@ruwa 'it was or became tender', r@xuwa 'it was or became loose', but even here the conjugational vowel u may be replaced by i and -uw- by -iy-, i.e. T@riya, r@xiya. However, -uuw (#/V) is fairly frequent, and, once again, the strong degree of muscular tension associated with gemination is characteristic of e.g. 9adúuw 'enemy' (m.), 9adúuwah 'enemy' (f.), fulúuw (one among several plural forms) 'foals', ?abúuwah 'paternity'. In general, however, relationships between ii, iy, iiy, uu, uw, uuw, etc., however interesting, are of less concern than the 'straightforward'

---

[1] Vowel successions are, of course, inadmissible.

use of ?álif, waaw, and yaa? to indicate the occurrence of long vowels in such forms as q@@l 'he said', Tuub 'brick(s)', fiil 'elephant', etc., or in non-ultimate syllables of fal@sTiiniíy, muusawíiy, samaawíiy, etc.

For the practical purposes of pronunciation, it is of great importance that the student should at all times maintain the distinction between short and long vowels (a(a), i(i), u(u)). The feature of length does not entail any significant difference of vowel quality— the long vowels are simply 'long fátħah/kásr@h/D@mmah'. The important feature is length and the long vowel must be pronounced at least twice as long as the short vowel. It is particularly difficult for English speakers—and Egyptians also have to learn—to pronounce vowels long in unaccented syllables, especially when these are at some remove from the accent, and the difficulty is compounded for the English learner by the need to retain the same vowel quality in successions of syllables, as in katabátaa[1,2] 'they (f.) both wrote'. Here now are some examples of contrast between short and long vowels and of forms in which long vowels occur pre- or post-tonically or both, at a greater or lesser distance from the accented or tonic syllable. In these and succeeding sections, the length feature is illustrated in the isolated word. Chapters 6 and 8 and Appendix A contain many examples within the phrase and sentence.

Short/long contrast: kátab 'he wrote'/káatab 'he corresponded', ǵ@ssal 'he washed (s.t.) thoroughly'/ǵ@ssáal 'laundryman', bálaħ 'dates'/samáa? 'sky', ʃáfah 'lip'/ʃáamah 'mole, birthmark', m@rr 'he passed by'/m@@rr 'passer-by; pedestrian', ?ámal 'hope'/ ?aamáal 'hopes', 9ínabah 'grape'/kitáabah 'writing', đúr@h 'sorghum' (cereal grass)/qúr@@ 'villages', Sífah 'quality; adjective'/síir@h 'conduct; way of life', sinn 'tooth; age'/siin 'letter s', sáhil (or sahl) 'smooth, even'/9adíil 'equal, like', kálimah 'word'/ jaríidah 'newspaper', tađkír@h (or tađk@r@h) 'permit'/sikkíinah 'knife', kúr@h 'sphere, ball'/Súur@h 'image, picture', rúsul 'messengers; prophets'/r@súul 'messenger; prophet', múdun 'cities'/ murúur 'passing (by); traffic', (li) yaktúba (subjunctive) '(let him) write'/Su9úubah 'difficulty', etc.

---

[1] An example of different accentual pattern between Egypt, i.e. Cairo, and elsewhere; see Chapter 7.

[2] Vernacular Arabic resists successions of CV syllables, and the comparatively exceptional Egyptian vernacular form kátabit 'she wrote' corresponds variously to kátbat or kátbit or even (i)ktíbat elsewhere.

Long vowel in unaccented syllable: ?aamáal 'hopes', r@?aa 'he saw', suuríyaa 'Syria', miSriiyáat 'Egyptian women; Egyptian-isms', wajadátaa 'they (f.) both found', muh@@r@bah 'fighting', fallaahúun 'peasants, peasant farmers', ǵ@@yátuhaa 'her object', baynáhumaa 'between the two of them', ?ahadúhumaa 'each of (the pair of) them', fal@sTiiniiyíin 'Palestinians', walaakinnáhu 'but he . . . ', etc.

Notes

1. The combination of consonant gemination and vowel lengthening will need special attention in e.g. fallaahúun, haśśaaśúun 'hashish addicts', etc. The hold of -śś- and -aa- should even be exaggerated before going on to the final accented syllable, whose vowel must also be given its due length.

2. Care must be taken not to shorten Arabic long vowels in the way that long vowels are contextually shortened in English (2.3, pp. 18–19). The English vowel of e.g. 'loose' is shorter than that of 'lose' but longer than that of 'looser', where it occurs before an unaccented syllable. This shortening must not be transferred to e.g. -uu- in Arabic múusaa 'Moses; (straight) razor', where vowel length approximately corresponds to that in southern standard English 'lose'.

5.3 Variants of fáthah; consonant and vowel

There are four principal variants of fáthah, one qualitatively front and three back. Variation between front a and back @ is a function of adjoining consonants, and as far as back variants are concerned, it is necessary to consider four further factors—the structure of the syllable in which the vowel occurs, the type of 'back consonant' involved, whether the consonant precedes or follows the vowel, and whether the vowel is short or long. First, however, let us specify those consonants which, in a strictly Classical pronunciation, when they are in post-pausal position and precede 'long fathah' in, let us say, the monosyllabic structure CVVC, require a back quality of open vowel similar to that of British 'hot', or, in imitation of some Arabic speakers, to that of a southern standard pronunciation of 'hart'. These consonants are Ð, T, D, S, r, q, x, ǵ. In most cases the names of the relevant Arabic letters supply appropriate examples, and it will be seen that the preceding 'back consonants' contrast with correlatives as follows:[1]

[1] saa? 'he/it became evil', 9aad 'he returned', and ǵ@@b 'he stayed away' have been used instead of the letter-names siin, 9ayn, and ǵ@yn.

	Front	Back
Non-emphatic/emphatic	Non-emphatic	Emphatic
	đaal	Đ@@?
	taa?	T@@?
	daal	D@@?
	saa?	S@@d
Liquid	Lateral	Trill
	laam	r@@?
Velar-cum-uvular (stop)	Velar	Uvular
	kaaf	q@@f
Guttural (fricative)	Pharyngal	Uvular
	ħaa?	x@@?
	9aad	ǵ@@b

The remaining letters carry the implication of front fátħah, as in their names or comparable lexical items: ?aal 'he reverted; family, clan', faa?, baa?, maa? 'water', waaw, ŧaa?, zaay, naam 'he slept, went to bed', śaa? 'he wanted', jaa? 'he came', haa?, yaa?.

The preceding formulation relates, of course, to an Egyptian strict Classical pronunciation and not to the facts of any form of vernacular Arabic. For example, in spoken Egyptian Arabic, x and ǵ are followed by aa, not @@, though in bedouin dialects—and there is a long tradition of reference to these dialects by urban speakers living in proximity to them—the uvular fricatives are associated with back fátħah. In such dialects, however, w is also linked with backness, whereas g and r fluctuate between the implication of frontness and backness. In the Egyptian vernacular, frontness or backness is unpredictable in association with r. In any form of spoken Arabic, the incidence of frontness and backness is, in fact, an 'overlaid' feature which does not respect syllable boundaries, but in the Classical pronunciation of our concern a conscious attempt is made to control this 'spreading' and to limit the front/back contrast to the domain of a single syllable. In Classical orthoepy primary importance is ascribed to the position of syllable-opening. Stock will shortly be taken of cases in which even a syllable-opening consonant is overridden by a following consonant, but, by and large, the quality of an open vowel is determined by the consonant opening the syllable in which the vowel occurs. It is time now to turn to the open vowel qualities which the learner must acquire.

(I) FRONT fátḥah

The three back variants should present little difficulty, but the front variant is likely to need practice. It is the most characteristic of the Arabic vowel sounds; it is of high frequency and occurs in all forms of the spoken language. Before practical hints are given as to its acquisition, mention should be made of three general considerations affecting English vowels which should provide the starting-points for learning Arabic counterparts. Firstly, individuals do not pronounce in exactly the same manner, and care must be taken not to base one's efforts on pronunciation that is idiosyncratic; secondly, language is subject to constant change, which gives rise, for example, to important generational differences of vowel pronunciation;[1] thirdly, English regional differences are mostly marked by vowel quality, and pronunciation instructions can be invalidated by the learner's use of a regional vowel in place of a standard form which all can identify.[2] The standard to which this book adheres is provided by the southern British 'accent' used, for example, by BBC news-readers. This is generally free from regionalism, affectation and other factors inimical to the present practical objective of teaching and learning an acceptable pronunciation of Classical Arabic. The learner is likely to be familiar with this 'standard' and at least to be able to imitate it, even if it does not correspond to his everyday habits of pronunciation. First, then, should be isolated the vowel of 'at' ('pat', 'bad', 'lack', etc.), which is a fully front vowel, between open and half-open (IPA symbol æ). This is too front and too open for Arabic front fátḥah—if possible, in order to perceive the difference, an Arab should be asked to pronounce his word man 'who' or lak 'to you' in place of the English words 'man' and 'lack' in the phrases 'a good *man*', 'a serious *lack*'.

---

[1] For example, many educated younger speakers of English today use an opener series of short vowels in, say, 'bid'/'bed'/'bad' than speakers of the preceding generation.

[2] Speakers from the north of England, for instance, or from, say, Gloucestershire and Oxfordshire, use too open a quality of vowel in 'bad' for our present purpose, Glaswegians use a vowel that is both too open and too back, whereas Devonians use the quality we are looking for and which also occurs in the 'standard'. It is not expected that the reader should be familiar with a wide range of regional English speech, but careful listening will provide excellent ear-training. A single evening's television programmes give scope for interesting comparisons between vowel sounds used by different types of speaker.

It becomes necessary, therefore, to locate a second English vowel, which, in conjunction with that of, say, 'bat', brackets the required Arabic quality. This is provided by the central vowel of e.g. 'Bert'. If one then takes the vowel of 'bat' as starting-point and introduces into it something of the vowel of 'Bert' (IPA symbol ɜ:), an acceptable Arabic baat 'he spent the night' should result, provided that the vowel is made sufficiently long. In the early stages, the learner is likely to make a vowel sounding too like English æ or ɜ:, as the case may be, and will need to adjust the sound until the correct quality is fixed in his perception and performance. On the vowel figure of 2.3 (p. 17), the three vowels in question may be plotted as in Fig. 14.

Other pairs and triplets for comparison and contrast are: Ar. ḍaat 'essence, nature; self', Eng. 'that'; Ar. jaab 'he brought', Eng. 'jab'; Ar. naas 'people', Eng. 'nurse'; Ar. ?aan 'it is time (that)', Eng. 'earn'; Ar. baad 'it perished, became extinct', Eng. 'bad', Eng. 'bird'; Ar. laam 'he blamed', Eng. 'lamb', Eng. 'learn'.

Arabic a should not, of course, be confused with English e of 'men', ɑ: of 'park', or eə of 'air'. The last of these is diphthongal, and it is well to note that Arabic vowels in general must not be diphthongized, at least in Classical pronunciation. A phonetic diphthong involves movement of the tongue or lips or both from the position required for one vowel in the direction of that required for another. In the case of eə, movement is from a half-open front position towards an open variety of central vowel, whence the notation e+ə. To guard against any such movement in Arabic, the learner should steady the tongue against the lower teeth and keep

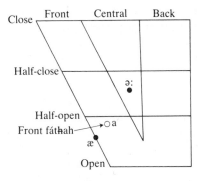

FIG. 14

tongue, jaw and lips absolutely still during the articulation of the vowel. A mirror is a useful aid against unwanted diphthongization. The second of the three examples, 'park', contains a long *back* vowel, which is evidently very wide of the *front* fátħah mark. As to the e of 'men', this is a front vowel but it is closer than mid and therefore too close as well as too front for Arabic a. At a pinch, in the case of students who pronounce too open a variety of English æ, the instruction can be given to them to make it 'sound a little more like' e, until an æ is achieved which can then be used as starting-point for the acquisition of Arabic a.

The importance has been stressed for English speakers of guarding against their tendency to weaken vowels in unaccented syllables and to maintain the same quality of front fátħah throughout successions of syllables containing it. It has been pointed out that the vowels of kánaza 'he buried; amassed' are to all intents and purposes identical in quality and, therefore, quite unlike those of English 'Canada' (kǽnədə). It is only in respect of length that the final vowel of e.g. sa?alátaa 'they (f.) both asked' differs from the other vowels of the form. A few further examples for practice, with and without the inclusion of other vowels, are: kátabah 'clerks', maktábah 'library; desk', ħayawaanáat 'animals', makáatib 'offices; libraries; desks', katabtúnna 'you (f.pl.) wrote'. The short/long difference must also be observed, cf. samm 'he poisoned; poison'/saam 'he offered for sale', fa?s 'hatchet, pickaxe'/faas 'Fez' (Moroccan city), ħámmam 'he heated; he bathed s.o. or s.t.'/ħammáam 'bath'/ħammaamáat 'baths'.

There is one noteworthy variant of front fátħah. It is the opener variety (close to cardinal a; see pp. 16–17) that occurs before and after the pharyngal fricatives ħ and 9, e.g. ħaśíiś 'grass; hashish', 9abd 'slave', baħt 'search(ing); research', ba9t 'despatching; resurrection', ħaal 'condition', 9aam 'year', baaħ 'it became known', baa9 'he sold; fathom'.[1]

(II) BACK fátħah

It is time now to turn to varieties of *back* fátħah, appropriate to co-occurrence of the vowel with one of the back consonants listed on

---

[1] There occurs some further minor variation, often individual, in the pronunciation of fátħah. Some Arabs, for example, tend to 'back' front fátħah after the labials b, m, and especially w.

p. 73. Mention has been made of three back variants, but if account is taken of the length of the vowel, the structure of the syllable in which it occurs, and the style of discourse, then the underlying distinction is twofold only. The third variant is required by high Classical style as opposed to the more relaxed style apt to less formal topics and interpersonal relationships. Let us first consider the stylistic factor. The educated Arab has available to him a variety of pronunciations, even Classical pronunciations, responding, for example, to the degree of literacy of a hearer or to the nature of the reading topic, and a more relaxed style entails greater or lesser vernacular influence of a regional kind. This influence involves among other things a reduction of emphasis in the four emphatic consonants and a degree of concomitant fronting of an accompanying open vowel. The result is that, in more relaxed style, there is little or no difference of implication as to back vowel quality among the eight consonants concerned (Ð, T, D, S, r, x, ǵ, q), although the influence of the emphatics on vowel quality is felt at a greater distance than in the case of the other consonants. It was earlier pointed out (pp. 27–30, 40–1) that fully emphatic articulation involves a position of the tongue that is not wholly amenable to simple description in terms of part and degree of tongue-raising, and it is this fact that explains the difference of acoustic impression in high Classical style between the vowels of, say, T@@b 'it ripened' and ǵ@@b 'he stayed away', with the latter more front in quality. For practical purposes, the back vowels of T@lab 'he asked' and T@@b may be equated with cardinal vowel ɒ,[1] which is approximately the vowel of standard southern English 'hot', whereas the vowel of ǵ@@b is similar to that of English 'park', calm', etc. In the more elevated style, ɒ is also distinguished from the more front, more centralized, short vowel ʌ of b@rr (bʌrr) 'land; open country', b@qq (bʌqq) 'bugs', etc., which is qualitatively that of the southern English standard vowel of 'bug'. The three vowel qualities may be plotted on the vowel figure as in Fig. 15.

In high Classical style, there is a clear difference between the ʌ variant of e.g. q@lb 'heart', r@dd 'he sent back', x@dd 'cheek', ǵ@ṣṣ 'he cheated' and the ɒ of e.g. T@rd 'expulsion; parcel', D@rb 'beating', Ð@ll 'he became', S@nf 'kind, sort', but in less formal style the vowels for all practical purposes coalesce in a quality closer

---

[1] The slightly rounded correlate of cardinal ɑ.

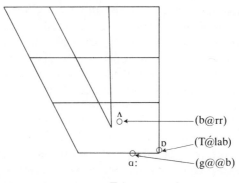

FIG. 15

to ʌ. The same is true of cases where the syllable is *closed* by a back consonant, as in b@qq 'bugs' and b@TT 'ducks'. All the preceding examples are of fátħah occurring in closed syllables, variously opened or closed by back consonants. In the open syllables of e.g. q@sama 'he divided', r@sama 'he drew', T@laba 'he asked', the relevant vowel is opener and backer, but again the quality ɒ is attributable to the syllable T@- in high Classical style only. More often, @ of q@sama, r@sama and T@laba shares the quality ɑː of @@ in e.g. n@@r 'fire', n@@T 'he hanged', etc., though it should perhaps be said once more that in high Classical the @@ of n@@T is backer than that of n@@r. The opener quality of short back fátħah is tied to the context in which the vowel follows the back consonant in an *open* syllable. A preceding short fátħah is of the closer ʌ-type when the consonant is intervocalic, as in e.g. h@r@ba (hʌrɑba) 'he fled', 9all@q@ (9allʌqɑ) 'he hung', etc., and this applies also to forms in which other vowels follow the back consonant, e.g. s@qima (sʌqima) 'he became ailing', f@xíir (fʌxiir) 'boastful', etc.[1] It will be noted that three different qualities of fátħah, two back and one front, occur in h@r@ba. In the more frequent, less formal style of pronunciation, the difference between closer (ʌ) and opener (ɑ(ː)) back varieties of the vowel is a function of vowel length (ʌ does not occur long) and of syllable type (the opener variety occurs in open syllables and the closer variety in closed). In high Classical style, the opener (and backer) variant ɒ occurs in the environment of the

---

[1] Round brackets here do not, of course, enclose IPA symbols, except in respect of the open vowels of our concern.

emphatic consonants. In the preceding examples, final short vowels
have been included, as they often are by teachers for demonstration
purposes; their typical pre-pausal omission entails, of course, difference of structure in the final syllable and the consequent use of
the same vowel quality in the two syllables of e.g. h@r@b (hʌrʌb),
ṣ@ġ@b (ṣʌġʌb) 'he made trouble; trouble'.

(iii) SOME PROBLEMS FOR ENGLISH SPEAKERS

In teaching foreign vowel sounds, reference to English qualities,
subject as these are to great regional variation, is inevitably
uncertain, whence the appeal explained earlier to the yardstick of a
standard form of English pronunciation. For example, the equating
of Arabic ɒ with the southern British vowel of 'hot' is likely to be of
little use to Americans and many Scots, whose corresponding vowel
is either too front or too rounded. The best practical advice may be
to ask the student to depress the back of the tongue with something
like a spatula and to say 'ah'. Sometimes Americans may be
successfully asked to pronounce the vowel of 'park' or the first
syllable of 'father' with the required slightly more back, unrounded
quality. Care must be taken by all learners not to round the vowel
ɑː, since rounding is likely to produce a vowel of the type in
(southern British) English 'raw', which, though back, is rounded
and only half-open, and not at all what is required. It has been said
that speakers of the southern British standard are unlikely to find
difficulty with any variant of back fátḥah, but British learners whose
speech contains regional characteristics may encounter problems.
The vowel of 'up', that is ʌ, for example, is often pronounced by
Londoners with too front a quality, and any such speaker should
make his vowel sound a little more like that of 'hot'. The variants ɑː
and ɒ are less likely to be difficult, though the vowel of 'park' is
often too front for ɑː in, for example, Yorkshire speech. However,
even ʌ is as a rule imitated successfully by northern speakers, whose
natural tendency when pronouncing, say, 'up' or 'but' will nevertheless be to use a vowel resembling that of southern 'put', that is,
an approximately half-close, back rounded vowel (Arabic D@m-
mah). This is often unrounded and markedly centralized in polite
northern speech, but this variant will equally not do for Arabic
purposes. Contrariwise, for many speakers from Liverpool the
pronunciation of e.g. 'bush' involves a vowel akin to that needed for
Arabic ʌ. For most northerners, the vowel of 'hot', made to sound a

little like the central vowel of 'bird', will pass muster, and the majority will in any case be capable of imitating the well-known southern standard on which earlier instructions have been based.

(IV) CONTEXTUAL INFLUENCES

It should be recalled that, in high Classical style, the quality of fátḥah depends upon the nature of the preceding syllable-opening consonant. Thus, long @@ before a back consonant closing a syllable which in turn is opened by a front consonant may appear, in the pronunciation of purists, as a diphthong, with the glide taking place between front and back fátḥah, e.g. l@@T (laɒT) 'it adhered', n@@r (naʌr) 'fire', bal@@g̣ (balaʌg̣)[1] 'message', man@@x (manaʌx)[1] 'climate', T@l@@q (Tɒlaʌq) 'divorce'. Such pronunciations, however, are essentially pedantic and the earlier pure or monophthongal form of @@ is in general satisfactory, though it is often somewhat fronted. Front fátḥah preceding a back consonant is more clearly in evidence when the consonant is not one of the emphatics and does not close a syllable, as in ʔináax@h (ʔinaːˀxɒh) 'making (camel) kneel', baláag̣@h (balaːˀg̣ɒh) 'eloquence'. This is especially noticeable when the consonant opening the syllable which contains long fátḥah is one entering into the front/back consonant contrast, as l (versus r) or d (versus D) in e.g. láaq@@ (laːˀqɑː) 'he met', dax@ltu 'I/you (s.m.) entered', laaT@fa (laːˀTɒfa) 'he treated kindly'. The occurrence of front fátḥah in these cases is relatable either to the length of the vowel or to the direct part played by the preceding consonant in the non-emphatic/ emphatic contrast, so that, when these conditions do not obtain, short fátḥah is typically pronounced with back quality in e.g. l@T@f(a)[2] 'he was kind', f@S@d(a) 'he bled s.o.', f@D@l(a) 'it was left over; he excelled', n@Ð@m(a) 'he threaded' (necklace), b@T@@lah 'bravery', b@Tin 'paunchy', f@Díilah 'virtue', 9@Ðíim 'mighty, great', etc. It should also be borne in mind that the corresponding long vowel is more likely to be pronounced with back quality in less formal (and more usual) style, e.g. ʔ@@x@r versus ʔáax@r 'other'.

The consonant r is of particular interest in respect of the quality of

---

[1] This is not, of course, a matter of vernacular influence, since the uvular fricatives are typically accompanied by front fátḥah in Egyptian vernacular Arabic.

[2] The pre-pausal omissible vowel is bracketed.

fátħah preceding it. When kásr@h follows r, as in e.g. báarid 'cold', then preceding fátħah cannot be back. This illustrates the typical 'spread' of such features as frontness and backness, although this is greatly more in evidence in the everyday spoken language, whereas its predominant limitation to the syllable is characteristic of high Classical pronunciation, which has to be consciously learned by its practitioners. Even the Classical rendering of such forms as muħ@@r@bah 'fighting' versus madaarísu 'schools', ʃ@@Tir 'cunning; clever' versus ʃáariϑ 'street; lawgiver', is as shown, and it would be the pronunciation of fátħah as back in the *final* syllable of muħ@@r@bah that would indicate vernacular pronunciation. Similarly, 'current' Classical pronunciation, so to say, includes b@r@d (bʌrʌd)[1] 'he filed' versus, say, baríid 'post, mail', ʃárϑii 'lawful', etc. Some speakers extend the feature to include cases of fátħah in a closed syllable, e.g. ?arríħ 'the wind', though ?@rríħ (?ʌ-) is to be preferred for Classical purposes. Nevertheless, front fátħah is the norm in words like dars 'lesson', bard 'cold', etc., in which specifically non-emphatic consonants are involved. We should perhaps recall the somewhat similar behaviour on a much smaller scale of the lateral correlate of r in the divine name (see p. 50).

Finally, it is not a necessary condition for the occurrence of back fátħah that it should be immediately contiguous to a back consonant, and the emphatics in particular influence the quality of a vowel at some distance. Consonants, too, are similarly affected, so that not only is fátħah back in the first syllable of e.g. m@nTiq 'logic' but n (and, for that matter, also m) is dark. Other comparable examples are t@mDii 'you (s.m.) sign', m@nSúub 'erected', m@nÐ@r 'view', and these could be greatly multiplied. In cases like b@sT@h 'extension', the pronunciation b@ST@h suggests a spelling other than the correct one, and Arabic speakers, if asked to identify the sulcal consonant, are likely to say 'It is really siin but sounds like S@@d'. They might even say the same of the initial consonant of s@x@T 'discontent' or of the medial consonant in ʒ@s@q 'twilight'. It is perfectly possible in the nature of things to pronounce a non-emphatic before a back vowel in such cases, but to do so is to resort, quite properly where appropriate, to the 'spelling pronunciations' that are part and parcel of Quranic orthoepy. In the foregoing

---

[1] The final consonant is of the 'mid-grade' spoken of on pp. 43–4.

examples, labial and uvular consonants precede fátħah, but in, say, tafxíim 'emphaticization' (of consonants) or tanśíiT 'encouragement', in the second of which the emphatic occurs at a distance, the contrast between non-emphatic t and emphatic T imposes a Classical pronunciation of front fátħah, though t@fxíim and t@nśíiT will certainly be heard. The mid-grade between non-emphasis and emphasis to which reference was made earlier (pp. 43–4) is almost certain to occur with s in s@x@T and ǵ@s@q and also in e.g. fas@TíiT 'tents, canopies', in the high Classical pronunciation of which the first fátħah must be front. The word is, however, comparatively infrequent, and in the contrasting case of the common (vernacular) forms m@bSúuT 'content' or b@SíiT 'simple; trifling', a conscious effort will be needed from the speaker in order to ensure 'proper', if somewhat pedantic, Classical pronunciation as mabsúuT and basíiT. The effect of the emphatic is felt regressively in these examples but progressively in e.g. vernacular ?@Sn@@f 'kinds', for which the Classical pronunciation is ?@Snáaf. There are many such examples that the learner should listen out for and be ready to question Arabic speakers about.

5.4 Variants of kásr@h

The striking variation of quality in the case of fátħah is less marked in the other vowels, kásr@h and D@mmah, since they themselves embody a distinction between front and back, which, it may be said in passing, is not always so clearly made in vernacular Arabic of a non-Egyptian kind. The two close vowels, however, do reveal a variety of quality which is a function of vowel length, of the structure of the syllable in which the vowel occurs, and of the organic formation of a preceding or following consonant. It will subsequently be seen that the qualitative differences between variants of kásr@h are strikingly parallel to those of D@mmah in terms of closeness and the contextual conditions of their occurrence.

(i) LONG kásr@h
There are three principal variants of kásr@h: a fully close front spread vowel (cardinal i, see pp. 15–17), a half-close front, somewhat centralized, spread vowel (IPA symbol ɪ), and a more front, slightly closer variety of the latter. The first of these

variants occurs only long, and it is this variant that is most likely to present English speakers with problems. The vowel of Arabic siin 'letter s' is fully close, whereas the tongue position of the similar English vowel in 'seen; scene', though front, is typically between half-close and close. In order to achieve the necessary additional raising of the front of the tongue, the learner is recommended to push with the tip against the lower teeth, spreading the lips vigorously and generally using greater muscular tension in the articulating organs. Another method, again with the use of considerable muscular tension, is to raise the tongue sufficiently to produce a fricative y (IPA symbol j), subsequently lowering the tongue just enough to eliminate the friction. The lips should be spread and the tip of the tongue pressed firmly against the lower teeth.

Some English speakers diphthongize the vowel of English 'see', 'fee', etc., in the form ii, especially when the vowel occurs final, as in the examples. This must not be done in Arabic, in particular in Classical pronunciation. Adherence to the instructions given in the preceding paragraph should suffice, but those who do pronounce such a diphthong in English should practise the Arabic vowel in isolation, taking care then and subsequently that there is no move-ment of tongue or jaw in the pronunciation of, say, Arabic fii 'in', which provides a direct contrast with English 'fee'. Other examples are tiin 'figs', matíin, 'strong, firm', diin 'religion', madíinah 'city', jalíis 'table companion', x@fíifah 'light' (s.f.).

(II) LONG kásr@h IN CONTEXT

Vowel glides do occur, of a predominantly central or central to open kind, on to and off emphatic, pharyngal and uvular consonants. These glides, however, are an inevitable concomitant of the organic formation of the consonants in question, and the attempt should always be made to pronounce ii in accordance with the previous instructions. Consonants and vowels do interact, however, as to their articulation. The learner may appreciate this from English if he adopts the tongue position for the initial consonant of, say, 'car' and then, without pronouncing the vowel, changes his mind and adopts the position for 'key'—he will feel the tongue drawn forward on the velum, which is, after all, a zone, not a point, of articulation. Similarly, in Arabic, the uvular articulation of x in e.g. xiim 'disposition' is fronter than in x@@f 'he was afraid'. At the same time, the consonants have a marked effect on the vowel. From the practical standpoint of pronunciation, the student should aim at making both consonant and vowel in accordance with earlier instructions, whereafter both glides and modified vowel quality will automatically follow. Any conscious attempt to 'add' a pre-vocalic and/or post-vocalic glide will result in defective performance. Thus, for example, whereas it is possible to adopt the posture for pharyngal ħ and 9 with little or no movement of the tongue perceptible in a mirror, nevertheless it is difficult to do so with the front of the tongue raised as for a close front vowel. The more open the tongue position, the easier these consonants are of demonstration. As a result, when ħ or 9 is preceded or followed by long kásr@h, the glides and quality of the vowel itself are inherent in the movements performed by the articulating organs in the speech process. Thus a diphthongal glide from opener to closer position is made following ħ in e.g. ħiin '(propitious) time', and ii not only does not attain the fully close position but is also somewhat centralized. The phonetic form is overall in marked vocalic contrast with e.g. the earlier diin 'religion'. When long kásr@h *precedes* the pharyngal, then an open type of central vowel glide on to the consonant is heard in e.g. riiħ 'wind', which contrasts in this respect with, say, kiis 'sack; pouch', where by comparison little movement is involved between vowel and final consonant.

Glides of an open type of central vowel are perhaps most noticeable on to and off the uvular plosive and the emphatic fricatives and plosives. Examples of these consonants preceding and following long kásr@h are as follows: qíila 'it was said', riiq 'saliva, spittle', d@qíiq 'thin, delicate'; Tiin 'clay', ?@SSíin 'China', biiD 'white' (pl.), Diiq 'narrowness', m@ríiD 'sick, ill', 9@Ðíim 'mighty', r@xíiS 'cheap' (s.m.), r@xíiS@h 'cheap' (s.f.), l@Tíif 'nice', muDíif 'host'. Useful articulatory and ear-training practice is provided by contrasting such examples with non-uvular and non-emphatic counterparts, e.g. qíila/kíila 'it was measured', riiq/diik 'cockerel', Diiq/diik, biiD/9iid 'festival', ?@SSíin/?assíin 'the letter s', m@ríiD/mufíid 'useful', 9@Ðíim/9adíim 'devoid (of)', etc.

(III) SHORT kásr@h IN CONTEXT

Short kásr@h, for its part, comprises two variants in accordance with the structure of the syllable in which the vowel occurs, and these variants are again subject to the same type of further variation as long kásr@h in the context of uvular, pharyngal and emphatic consonants. The principal short variant occurs in closed syllables and is a half-close front, somewhat centralized, spread vowel closely similar to that of English 'sit' or 'sin'. The second variant is a fronter, slightly closer version of the first, and occurs with some speakers in open syllables, especially when final, as in bíhi 'with him'. The first variant occurs in e.g. bint 'girl', jins 'species, class', ?istidláal 'reasoning, deduction', ħawáadiŧ 'happenings; accidents', and the second in miláff 'reel; file, folder', filáaħah 'tilling', mina lmuɡallimíin 'from the teachers', etc. The two co-occur in e.g. silsílah 'chain', filízz 'non-precious metal'. It should be said that not all speakers clearly distinguish between the two variants. In junction with the uvulars, pharyngals and emphatics, the variants tend in any case to fall together and short kásr@h has a centralized and rather more open quality than elsewhere, especially in the pharyngal and emphatic contexts. Examples are: ɡilm 'knowledge, science', díqq@h 'thinness; fineness', m@r@@wiħ 'fans, ventilators', S@náa?iɡ 'arts, skills', d@q@@?iq 'intricacies; minutes', xilT 'ingredient', miSr 'Egypt', Didd 'against', Tibb 'medicine', x@@liS 'pure, unadulterated', múxliS 'sincere; loyal', mur@@biT 'marabout, holy man', muxlíS@h 'sincere; loyal' (s.f.), ɡiláaq@h 'strap, hanger', S@@líħah 'sound, solid' (s.f.), Sinaaɡíiy 'artificial'.

With the principal short variant identified as i_1 and the subsidiary (in part, optional) variant as i_2, the three variants may be presented on the vowel figure, together with relevant English vowel sounds, as in Fig. 16.

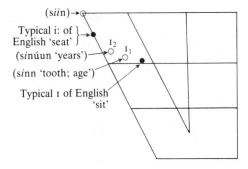

FIG. 16

5.5 Variants of D@mmah

As with kásr@h, so with D@mmah, there are three principal
variants, whose distribution is noticeably parallel to that of the front
vowel variants. D@mmah is, of course, a close back rounded vowel,
fully close (as cardinal u) when long, and approximately half-close
when short. The short variants are essentially two in number, of
which the principal one, like that of kásr@h, is a half-close vowel, as
in e.g. jubn 'cheese', whereas its optional subsidiary is closer,
especially when final, as in e.g. zawjátuhu 'his wife'.

(i) LONG D@mmah

The nearest English vowel sound to that of long D@mmah (uu) is
that of 'food' or 'boot', but, even in the southern standard, the
tongue position for this vowel is somewhat centralized and less than
fully close, whereas in the speech of many younger people
nowadays, as well as in a number of regional dialects, it is markedly
fronted, in a way that is quite unacceptable in Arabic. At the same
time, the Arabic vowel is characterized by stronger lip-rounding
and lip-protrusion than in the English case. The differences appear
quite clearly between, say, Arabic nuun 'letter n' and English
'noon', Arabic tuum 'garlic' and English 'doom'. The necessary
quality can usually be obtained by strongly rounding and protruding
the lips, with a simultaneous all-round increase in muscular tension.
Another method of acquisition is to start from the position of w- in,
say, 'war', omitting the vowel and prolonging the labio-velar
semivowel, at the same time increasing lip-rounding and
protrusion.

Some English speakers diphthongize the relevant English vowel,
especially when final, as in 'too' or 'blue'. The first element of this
diphthong typically has the quality of the southern standard vowel
in 'put' (IPA symbol ʊ), and the subsequent glide is to a closer
vowel position, with a concomitant increase in lip-rounding. This
must, of course, be avoided in Arabic, and, when practising the
vowel in isolation, care must be taken to ensure that there is no
movement of tongue, jaw or lips. Further examples of long D@m-
mah in various contexts are as follows: fuul 'beans', ɖuu 'owner of;
endowed with', buyúut 'houses; tents; verses', falúuw 'colt, foal',
janúub 'south', mamnúu9 'forbidden', falúukah 'felucca, boat',

w@S@luu 'they arrived', D@r@búuni 'they beat me', muɡallimúun 'teachers', yataɡallamúuna 'they learn'.

(II) SHORT D@mmah IN CONTEXT

The two short variants differ precisely in the manner of those of kásr@h between opener and closer quality, the former associated with closed syllables, the latter optionally with open. The basic short quality is that of the vowel in the southern standard pronunciation of English 'put', 'foot', etc.[1] (IPA symbol ʊ). The closer quality ($ʊ_2$), when it occurs, approaches that of the vowel in English 'boot', but the vowel is, of course, shorter. Examples are: rukn 'prop; corner', múddah 'period', túmma 'then', múflis 'bankrupt', r@jul 'man', dukkáan 'shop', húwa 'he', kutáyb 'booklet', muw@DD@f 'official', fataħáthu 'she opened it (m.)'.

The effect of back consonants, notably uvulars, pharyngals and emphatics, which have been seen to play an important part in determining the quality of fátħah and kásr@h in a given case, is greatly reduced, as far as D@mmah is concerned. Thus the quality of the short vowel in the following examples is for all practical purposes the same as that already indicated above: ɡumr 'life', qúbbah 'dome', Đulm 'cruelty, injustice', Suɭb 'hard', xuDr 'green' (pl.), muĐ@llil 'shady'. In general, the need is, as in the case of kásr@h, to aim at the correct pronunciation of consonant and vowel, whereafter any vocalic modification will automatically ensue. It is only in the case of long D@mmah following an emphatic that a noticeably opener quality of the vowel may be heard than that associated with it elsewhere, but the difference is minimal. Examples are Tuub 'bricks' (contrast tuub 'repent!' (s.m.)), Suur 'Tyre' (versus suur 'wall; enclosure').

The variants of D@mmah, together with relevant English vowels, may be plotted on the vowel figure as in Fig. 17.

5.6 'Diphthongs'

A brief addendum should perhaps be made on the topic of voluntarily made vowel glides or combinations of vowel sound in a single syllable, though, strictly speaking, diphthongs are no part of Classi-

---

[1] For some very brief remarks concerning the regional pronunciation of this vowel in the north of England, see p. 79.

The Arabic Vowels

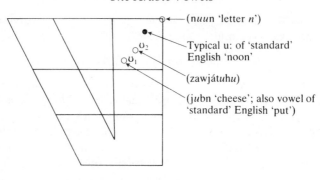

FIG. 17

cal Arabic pronunciation. It may nevertheless happen that speakers without training in strict Classical orthoepy may allow their performance to be influenced by vernacular habits, and it is certainly true that phonetic diphthongs do occur in Egyptian vernacular Arabic, though here, too, they are phonetic 'accidents' rather than part of the systematic phonology of the language. For example, the vowel i is regularly elided in the junction of, say, śáayil 'carrying' and -u 'it' (m.), and the consequent form śaaylu is subject further to shortening of the long vowel (aa) in a closed syllable, whence the resultant form śáylu 'carrying it'. The pronunciation of the form, which is, of course, excluded from the Classical language, is likely to involve a pronunciation of y which is vocalic and hence a phonetically diphthongal form of vowel in the first syllable. This may well be undesirably carried over by some speakers to their pronunciation of e.g. CA sayf 'sword', kayl 'measure', D@yf 'guest', etc., with the quality of fáthah determined by context in the manner already explained and y pronounced with the closest quality of the vowel kásr@h, i.e. without the palatal characteristics of consonantal y. Similarly, with w in e.g. kawm 'heap', q@wm 'people', tawr 'ox', S@wǵ 'fashioning, shaping', etc., a glide may be performed by such speakers to the closest quality of D@mmah, without the strong lip-rounding and protrusion appropriate to the consonantal articulation of w.

It is only after short fáthah and before y and w that this diphthongal realization of ay and aw may sometimes be heard in Classical pronunciation. When final, the consonantal characteristics of palatal friction (y) and lip-rounding and protrusion (w), both accompanied by considerable muscular tension, are usually perceived in e.g. ?ay 'i.e., that is', and ?aw 'or', and also in cases where the consonant follows long fátḥah, as in ?aay 'tokens; wonders; Quranic verses', waaw 'letter w'. By contrast, in the vernacular language, the latter sequences give rise in forms like šaay 'tea', kakáaw 'cocoa' to 'imperfect diphthongs', in which the second element (y, w) is pronounced as a vowel but the first is lengthened in a way that does not belong to a normally constituted diphthong.

It need hardly be said, in conclusion, that the English diphthongs of e.g. 'bait' and 'life' will not do for a Classical pronunciation of e.g. bayt 'house' and S@yf 'summer', nor that of, say, 'lout' for CA mawt 'death' or S@wt 'sound; voice', though in some dialects diphthongs occur which are closer to the English sounds.

6

JUNCTIONS

6.1 Morphological assimilations

Assimilation is the influence of one consonant on a neighbouring consonant, *regressive* when the first consonant is influenced by the second, *progressive* when the second is influenced by the first. Assimilations are widespread in vernacular Arabic and include among others the regressive assimilation as to voice of voiced b to voiceless t in e.g. sabt 'sabbath', of d to t in e.g. sajádt 'I prostrated myself', of Z to t in ḥaf@Zt 'I kept, I guarded', etc., but, as a general principle, these assimilations are best avoided in Classical pronunciation and voice should continue through the voiced consonant. We do not, therefore, need to concern ourselves with assimilations of this kind.

The regressive case of 'homorganic n' in the sequence -nC- was noted earlier (pp. 50–1) *within words*, but between words and particles there regularly occurs the assimilation of n to consonants other than those cited earlier. Thus, the particle min may be heard in the form mir before r, mil before l and mim before m, as in mir r@ḥmáti lláah 'from the mercy of God', mil lúndun 'from London', mímmaa (< min maa) 'from that which'.[1] mimmaa and mimman (< min man) 'from who(m)' are recognized in writing, where particle and pronoun are written as a single form with geminated m. Similarly, the 'nominalizing' particle ?an[2] takes the form ?al before the negative particle laa and, once again, ?allaa (< ?an laa) is recognized in Arabic writing, as in q@@la láhu ?alláa yaðhába 'He told him not to go'. Finally, though in Quranic chant only, the meeting of n and y across a word-boundary results in a palatal nasal (IPA symbol ɲ), which is the final sound of French *montagne* and the medial sound of French *agneau*, Spanish *año*, Italian *ogni*, etc.,

---

[1] As in the first speech of the old man in the reading passage 'The King and the Ancient' in Appendix A, p. 151.

[2] Which introduces, for example, an object complement clause in q@@la láhu ?an yaðhába 'He told him to go'.

as in báytuɲ yúskan 'a house that is lived in' or 'a habitable house'. It may be noticed in passing that the vowel preceding ɲ is strongly nasalized in this context and nuun 'letter n' is given the name núunu lɣúnnah 'nasalization nuun', often dubbed, because of the similarity of roots involved, 'the nuun of singing'.

The above assimilations involving n are, however, rare in comparison with those affecting l of the article, which is totally assimilated to the following noun-initial consonant if this is dento-alveolar, or if it is palato-alveolar ʃ. The learner should from the outset devote much practice to this assimilatory type, if only because it is so frequent. The noun-initial consonants concerned are termed in Arabic ?alħurúufu ʃʃamsíiyah 'the sun letters', among which the ʃ of ʃams 'sun' figures as something of a non-dento-alveolar 'odd man out', whereas the remaining labials, palatals (including palato-alveolar j), velars, uvulars, pharyngals and glottals, are labelled ?alħurúufu lq@m@ríiyah 'the moon letters', identified by the q of ?alq@m@r 'the moon', which does not permit assimilation. Membership of the two groups is numerically equal (14 each), and they are as follows:

'Sun' letters

t	?attáanii 'the second, the other'
d	?addawabáan '(the) melting'
D	?@DD@rf 'elegance'
t	?att@Sríih 'the declaration; the permit'
d	?add@r@jah 'the step; the grade'
T	?@TT@@lib 'the student'
D	?@DDúɡf 'weakness'
s	?assámak '(the) fish'
z	?azzíinah '(the) embellishment'
S	?@SSíin 'China'
r	?arriwáayah 'the story; the play'
l	?alliwáa? 'the flag'
n	?annúwab 'the misfortunes'
ʃ	?aʃʃayT@@n 'the Devil, Satan'

'Moon' letters

f	?alfurúuɡ 'the branches'
b	?albustáan 'the garden'
m	?almáwj 'the waves, breakers'
w	?alw@r@q@h 'the leaf; the sheet'
j	?aljamáaɡah 'the group (of people)'
y	?alyamíin 'the right side; the right hand'
k	?alk@r@@mah 'nobility'
q	?alqúds 'Jerusalem'
x	?alx@rTúuʃ 'the cartridge'
ɣ	?alɣ@ríiq 'the drowned man'
ħ	?alħiláaq@h 'shaving; the barber's trade'
ɡ	?alɡúnSur 'the race, breed'
h	?alhiláal 'the crescent; the new moon'
?	?al?áan 'now'.

Another important category of morphological junctions entailing assimilation, this time progressive for the most part and notably less frequent than the article, involves the infixed -t- of derived form VIII of the verb. Assimilations of this type are more widespread in the vernacular language, in which other derived forms are also concerned, but these need not detain us. The following implications of -Ct- junction appertain to Classical Arabic.

The emphatics S, D, T, Ḍ: the assimilation of t for emphasis occurs in all cases. These assimilations are indicated in written Arabic, and, in cases of gemination, the doubled letter is written with šáddah.

> S+t = ST, e.g. ?iST@na9 'he commissioned s.t.', ?iST@laḥ 'he accepted s.t.'
> D+t = DT, e.g. ?iDT@r@b 'he became agitated', ?iDT@la9 'he was proficient (in)'.
> T+t = TT, e.g. ?iTT@la9 'he looked', ?iTT@r@ḥ 'he flung away'.

The junction of Ḍ and t is rare, but when it does occur, assimilation is complete, for voice, emphasis and non-sulcal articulation, i.e.

> Ḍ+t = ḌḌ, e.g. ?iḌḌ@lam 'he was wronged'.

The non-emphatics z, d, ḍ: in the cases of z and d, assimilation is for voice, i.e.

> z+t = zd, e.g. ?izdáḥam 'it became crowded', ?izdáad 'it increased'.
> d+t = dd, ?iddá9am 'he supported himself', ?iddá9aa 'he alleged'.

In the case of ḍ+t, assimilation is, optionally, either for both voice and non-sulcal articulation (ḍḍ) or for a combination of progressive assimilation for voice and regressive assimilation for plosive articulation (dd), i.e.

> ḍ+t = either ḍḍ or dd, e.g. ?iḍḍák@r or ?iddák@r 'he remembered', ?iḍḍ@x@r or ?idd@x@r 'he preserved'.

These non-emphatic assimilations are also embodied in the Arabic written forms.

6.2 hamzátu lw@Sl

No CA form may begin with a consonant cluster, nor may there occur sequences of more than two consonants. In order to obviate these conditions, a cluster is preceded in certain grammatical forms and a few individual words by hamz(ah)+vowel, i.e. ?VCC-. This hámzah is known as hamzátu lw@Sl 'the hámzah of linking', and is omitted, together with the following vowel, after a word ending in a vowel, i.e. $-C_1V_1+C_2V_2C_3-$ = $C_1V_1C_3$ (where C_2 is hamzátu lw@Sl and V_2 the 'prop' vowel), e.g. ŧám@ru+?ann@xl = ŧám@ru nn@xl 'the fruit of the palm'. Certain morphologically long vowels preceding w@Sl are shortened in junction, so that the formula applies to both short and (most cases of) long V_1. For practical purposes of fluency and the proper observation of Arabic rhythm, it is of the utmost importance to practise running the final vowel of the preceding word on to the consonant following the elided hamz(ah)+vowel, as in the name itself hamzátu lw@Sl. Any consonant-ending word preceding hamzátu lw@Sl is given a final anaptyctic vowel in order to obviate the hypothetical three-consonant sequence entailed by the elision of hamz(ah)+vowel, so that, in amplification of the earlier statement, it should be said that hamzátu lw@Sl and the following vowel are elided when not post-pausal.

Undoubtedly the most important of the categories containing w@Sl is the article and those forms like ?@ll@@h 'Allah, God', and the relative pronoun ?alládii and the related forms which contain the article. Thereafter come the past tense, the imperative and the verbal noun of form VII and the following derived forms of the verb, e.g. (form VIII) ?ijtáma9 'it assembled', ?ijtámi9 'assemble!', ?ijtimáa9 'assembly'. Thirdly, there is the imperative of the simple form of the verb, e.g. ?íqr@? 'read!', as in ?únÐur w@ qr@? 'look and read!'. Lastly, the numeral ?iŧnáani 'two' and its related case and gender variants, as well as the particular nouns ?ism 'name', ?ibn 'son', ?íbnah 'daughter', ?ist 'buttock', ?ímr@? 'man' (?alm@r?, with the article), ?imr@?ah 'woman' (?alm@r?ah, with the article).

We shall not illustrate all of these categories, most of which are exemplified in the reading passages in Appendix A, but shall concentrate, as a most important means of achieving fluency in reading (and, indeed, speaking), on the elision of hamzátu lw@Sl in words containing the article and on the assimilation or non-assimilation, as the case may be, of l to the 'sun' and 'moon' letters. The learner should practise these features in a variety of grammatical contexts, for example in relation to non-initial nouns in the so-called 'construct' phrase, in noun–adjective phrases, in demonstrative phrases, in prepositional phrases, in post-verbal subject nouns, and so on, and in combinations of such structures. The following is a selection drawn mostly from the aforementioned reading passages, and the student can add freely to them from his own further reading. In this, as in all matters of pronunciation learning, a cassette recorder, used to record and play back both native speaker performance and the student's imitation of it, is an invaluable aid.

The first examples are of non-assimilation:

q@líilu l?ádab 'ill-mannered'
muh@@r@batu l?ummíiyah[1] 'combating illiteracy'
mina[2] l&@@báti lq@ríibah 'from the near-by wood'
huzmátu lh@T@bi háadih(i)[1] 'this bundle of wood'
min šiddáti lbárd 'from the extreme cold'
?áhadu l9@S@@fíir 'one of the little birds'
?ila(a)[3] lyáwm 'up to the day, up to today'
fii báyti lj@@r 'in the neighbour's house'
fii ?íhda(a)[3] lmúdun 'in one of the towns'
?alqir@@?átu wa lkitáabah[1] 'reading and writing'
ta9rífu lkaláam 'she knows how to speak' (said of a parrot)
(záwjii) yuhsínu lqir@@?ah '(my husband) can read well'
li ta9líimi lfallaahíina wa l9ummáal 'for the instruction of (the)
    agricultural workers and artisans'
wikaalátu l?anbáa?i l9@r@bíiyah 'the Arab News Agency'

The following are examples of assimilation:

S@@híbu ddukkáan 'the shop-owner'
Sundúuqu ttúrs '(the) gearbox'
?@TT@@híru ttiyáab 'the irreproachable one'
?assaalífu ddíkr 'the aforementioned'
q@líilu ssimáa9 'hard of hearing'

---

[1] Pausal forms are dealt with in 6.3.
[2] For the anaptyctic vowel -a with min, see below under examples of anaptyxis before w@Sl.
[3] With shortening of a long vowel before w@Sl.

9ílmu ssam9iiyáat 'acoustics'
t@m@ru nn@xl 'the fruit of the palm'
háad@(@) rr@jul 'this man'
9ala(a) zzamáan 'always'
ba9d@ DDúhr 'in the afternoon, this afternoon'
min báyti ssáariq 'from the thief's house'
bú9du SSíit 'fame'
háada(a) śś@hr 'this month'
bí smi lláah 'in the name of God'
śarikátu TT@y@r@@ni llubnaaníiyah 'the Lebanese Aviation
    Company'
?alhuSúulu 9ala(a) tt@rxíiS 'obtaining permission'
ta9ajjába śśáyxu min kaláamih 'the old man marvelled at his words'
láa yazáalu ttahqíiqu mustamírr@n 'the inquiry is still continuing'.

The following contain a mixture of assimilation and non-
assimilation:

fii haadíhi lmadaarísi llaylíiyah 'in these night-schools'
fi(i) lhaajáti śśadíidah 'in (the) extreme need'
?iijáadu TT@@?ir@@ti lm@Tlúubah 'obtaining the aircraft
    requested'
ma9@ DD@9íifi l9@ql 'with the feeble-minded one'
(fii ?awaaxíri) háada(a) śś@hri lmúqbil '(at the end of) this coming
    month'
r@?aa ?anna ssayy@@r@ta lw@@qífata ?amáama lbáyt... 'he saw
    that the car standing in front of the house...'

The following are examples of vowel-shortening in particles and
demonstratives before w@Sl:

(fii)   fi lb@hr 'on *or* in the sea'
(9alaa) 9ala lfir@@ś 'on the bed *or* in bed'
(maa)   má smuk? 'what is your name?'
(haadaa) háada nn@xl 'this palm'
(lammaa) lámm@ qt@r@ba ssáyyid... 'when Mr... approached'.

Final vowel-length is maintained in the fairly rare case of masculine
sound plural nouns occurring before w@Sl, e.g. mudarrísuu lmáktab 'the school('s) teachers', which contrasts with singular mudar-
rísu lmáktab.

    When w@Sl is no longer post-pausal and the preceding word ends in a consonant, the elision of hamz(ah) and the following vowel entails a potential three-consonant succession, which is obviated by the introduction of an anaptyctic vowel after the word-final consonant. This vowel is normally -i, but -a exceptionally occurs in the case of the particle min. The occurrence of -u, restricted to the context of certain pronominal suffixes, is explained subsequently. Anaptyctic -i and -a are indicated by italic fount in the following examples:

D@@9at*i* lbab@ǵ@@? (< D@@9at+?albab@ǵ@@?) 'the parrot was lost'

(sa?aláhu) 9an*i* lbab@ǵ@@? '(he asked him) about the parrot'

q@d*i* ŝt@r@t 'it (f.) has already bought'

(?alħayáatu) ?aw*i* lmáwt '(life) or death'

kalimátun*i* xt@rtah(u) 'a word you chose (it)'

wa káanat*i* lkalimátu (ŝáy?an ?@@x@r) 'and the word was (something else)'

(q@d) rúfi9at*i* sti9dáadan (li . . .) 'it (f.) had (already) been raised in readiness (for . . .)'

(w@D@9a kulla waaħídin) min*a* lqismáyn '(he placed each (one)) of the two pieces'

Note

The anaptyctic vowels do not appear to count for the purpose of accentuation, and may be regarded for this purpose as belonging to the following word. For accentuation, see Chapter 7.

Anaptyctic -u occurs after the second and third person plural suffixes -kum and -hum, which are subject to a process of close-vowel harmony in successive syllables, within which process the anaptyctic vowel is included. Thus, in baytúhum 'their house', with -u- repeated in the nominative case-ending of baytu and also in the suffix, anaptyctic -u is added before w@Sl of e.g. ?attáanii, i.e. baytúhumu ttáanii 'their second house'.

All third person suffixes except the third singular feminine -haa, which contains the open vowel, i.e. -hu (s.m.), -humaa (dual), -hum (third pl.m.), -hunna (third pl.f.), are subject to close-vowel harmony. Following -i-, -ii- or -ay-, the suffixes take the forms -hi, -himaa, -him and -hinna, e.g.

?iláyhi (< ?ilaa+-hu) 'to him'
min 9aynáyhi 'from his eyes'

bi ?asnaaníhi 'with his teeth'
bíhimaa 'with both of them'
min baytihínna 'from their (f.) house'.

An anaptyctic vowel following -him also takes the form -i, e.g.

bi baytíhimi ttáanii 'in their second house'.

An example of vowel harmony and of anaptyxis in the case of the second person plural suffix -kum is

baytúkumu ttáanii 'your (pl.) second house'.

When a w@Sl-beginning noun, e.g. ?ijtimáa9 'meeting, assembly', ?ism 'name', is prefixed with the article, the form taken by the latter is ?al- post-pausally and l- elsewhere. A three-consonant sequence comprising l of the article and the first two consonants of the noun is obviated by the insertion of an anaptyctic vowel after l. Thus,

1. ǂ?ijtimáa9
2. ǂ?aljtimaa9 > ǂ?alijtimáa9
3. r@?aa lijtimáa9 'he witnessed the meeting'
   r@?yu lijtimáa9 'the opinion of the meeting'.

If article-prefixed nouns of this kind follow a consonant, then potentially a four-consonant cluster arises from the elision of both instances of hamzátu lw@Sl, e.g. *(?uktu)b lsm 'write the name!' In
                                        1 23 4
such cases, the usual anaptyctic vowel is inserted after the first consonant (b in the example) as well as the anaptyctic vowel following l, i.e. ?úktubi lísm. This, is, however, something of a puzzle, since the anaptyctic vowel of lism would alone seem to obviate any unacceptable pattern of consonant succession, i.e. *?uktub lism. The particle min, followed by anaptyctic -a, behaves similarly, e.g. mina lísm 'from the name', mina lijtimáa9 'from the meeting'.

The treatment of a long vowel final in the word preceding the above cases of 'double w@Sl' varies with the grammatical category of the item to which the long vowel belongs. It is shortened in the case of particles but notably not that of verbs. Contrast, for example,

fi lijtimáa9 (< fii+lijtimáa9) 'in the assembly'
9ala littiħáad (< 9alaa+littiħáad) 'on unity'

with
r@?aa lijtimáa9 'he saw the assembly'
lam yu****Ð****híruu littiⱨáad 'they did not show unity'
kay yu****Ð****hír@@ littiⱨáad 'so that they both show unity'.

6.3 Final unvoicing

Mention has been made of the frequent unvoicing of final voiced
consonants and of the feature of q@lq@lah, which, it should be
added, does not apply exclusively to word-final position, since the
five consonants, b, d, j, T, q, are treated in the same way when
syllable-final in medial position, e.g. ?ibᵒtidáa? 'start', ?iqᵒtisáam
'dividing, distributing', etc. But Quranic recitation is not our
objective, however directly the Classical pronunciation which *is* our
concern is traceable to Quranic orthoepy, and the voiced consonants of the q@lq@lah-series are far from being the only ones
subject to final unvoicing in styles other than Quranic recitation.
There are two types of this unvoicing. Firstly, all voiced consonants
with the exception of 9, and, with some speakers, also ǧ, are often
weakly articulated and partially unvoiced pre-pausally. Examples
are baab̥ 'door; chapter', t@qlíid̥ 'imitation', f@rrúuj̥ 'pullet',
taⱨmíiD 'souring; (photographic) development', ?alf@@Ð̥ (or
?alf@@Z̥) 'expressions; pronunciations', qúd̥ad̥ 'feathers (of
arrow), faaz̥ 'he triumphed', s@@ǧ̥ (more often, s@@ǧ̥) 'he swal-
lowed'. Unvoicing is not as a rule complete in these cases. The first
part of the consonant tends to be voiced and unvoicing limited to the
final transition to silence (or pause). This type of unvoicing applies
most noticeably to *post-vocalic* occurrence of the consonants concerned, although it does also occur *post-consonantally*, especially
where resonants are involved, e.g. D@rb̥ 'striking', 9umẙ 'blind'
(pl.), q@dr̥ 'amount; rank', or after a voiceless consonant, e.g.
q@Sd̥ 'purpose'. This progressive assimilation of a final voiced
consonant to a preceding voiceless one is very common. In vernacular Egyptian Arabic, final clusters tend to be voiceless or voiced *as a
whole*, and this feature is frequently carried over to Classical
pronunciation. The unvoicing is particularly noticeable with final
liquids, semivowels and the bilabial nasal, e.g. r@Tl̥[1] 'pound
(weight)', ⱨusn̥ 'beauty', qism̥ 'portion; department', 9afw̥ 'efface-
ment; pardon', etc. The voicing of the final consonant in such cases

---

[1] A voiceless lateral is the sound of Welsh *ll* in e.g. 'Llanelli'.

would tend to be regarded as rather pedantic or appropriate to the speech of a teacher taking pains to enunciate words very clearly for the benefit of pupils. The articulation of final consonants subject to this process of assimilation may be performed quite vigorously in some cases, so that, for example, r in e.g. q@Sr 'shortness; castle' may well be trilled as well as voiceless, and this positive strength of articulation also sets this type of unvoicing off from the first type of *weakly* articulated, partially unvoiced final consonants.

The weakness of articulation just referred to is reminiscent of English lenis (weak) consonants as opposed to fortis (strong) counterparts. Fortis consonants are more often spoken of as 'voiceless' and lenis consonants as 'voiced', although, in truth, it is only between voiced sounds and especially between vowels that voiced consonants proper may safely be assumed to occur in English pronunciation. Elsewhere, the stops b and d, for example, are very weakly articulated, with little or no voicing in e.g. 'bad' or 'bard', 'dab' or 'daub'. Although *final* consonant articulation of this kind will pass muster in Arabic, it is important to guard against transferring this habit to *initial* voiced consonants in Arabic. Thus, the final phase of -b in e.g. baab may be like a very weakly articulated p, but not so the first phase of initial b-. To avoid excessive unvoicing, aim at 'pre-voicing' the consonant, at introducing the buzz of voice from its inception, at least in 'classical' pronunciation.

6.4 Pausal forms

The implications for pronunciation of certain junctions remaining to be specified relate first and foremost to words that occur in apocopated form before pause, that is, predominantly, final in the phrase and sentence. Pausal forms must be learned before an Arabic sentence can be pronounced properly. The isolated word, occurring, for example, in a spoken word-list, is also associated with pause and is primarily used in pausal form, but full forms are also often used for demonstration purposes. In discourse, it should not be expected that pause will always neatly correlate with grammatical phrasal divisions nor that the most appropriate divisions are always observed by speakers or readers, but the principle should always be followed that, wherever a pause is made, the preceding word should be pronounced in its pausal form. These forms are derivable from the following rules:

(i) a final short vowel, for example those of case, tense and
     mood, is omitted, e.g. kátab(a) 'he wrote', yáktub(u) 'he
     writes', (li?an) yáktub(a) '(so that) he may write', fii
     madáaris(a) 'in schools', fi lbáyt(i) 'in the house';

(ii) the sign of the indefinite, i.e. nunation (-n), is omitted,
     together with the preceding vowel, in the nominative (-un)
     and genitive (-in) cases of nouns and adjectives, e.g.
     bayt(un), fii báyt(in), mundu zámanin wajíiz(in) 'a little
     while ago', etc.;

(iii) accusative -an may be replaced by long fátħah (-aa), e.g.
     ?aɠT@@hu ɠiśríina diin@@r@@ 'he gave him 20 dinars',
     with the exception of adverbial forms like ?áyD@n 'also',
     ħáalan 'at once', etc.;

(iv) the feminine singular and unit ending táa?(un) m@rbúuT@h
     is replaced by -h in all three cases and both states of
     definiteness, i.e. -tun/-tan-/tin > -h, whence the Arabic writ-
     ten device ة , which combines features of t and h, e.g.
     jamíilah (< jamiilátun) 'beautiful' (s.f.), (fátaħat)
     madaarísa laylíiyah (< layliiyátan) '(it (f.) opened) night-
     schools', etc., fi ljunáynah (< junaynáti) 'in the little
     garden'.

In the following passage, used again for intonation purposes at
the end of Chapter 8, the pauses—indicated by the solidus—are
those made originally by a speaker trained in the high Classical
tradition, but they by no means represent the only possibilities for
pause, and indeed, in some cases—indicated by a square bracket
enclosing the solidus—improvement might be made by pausing at a
later point. Round brackets enclose elements omitted in pause.

?unśí?at jamɠiiyátun fii ?íħda lmúdun(i) / ɠ@@yátuhaa
muħ@@r@batu l?ummíiyah(-ti) / fa fátaħat haadíhi ljamɠíiyah(-tu)
[/] madaarísa layliiyátan fi lqúr@@ wa lmúdun(i) / li taɠlíimi
lfallaaħíina wa lɠummáal(i) [/ ?a]lqir@@?áta wa lkitáabah(-ta). / fa
?@rsálat yáwman mufattíśan ?ilaa ?íħda lqúr@@ / yaħmílu
hadáayaa li lladíina yataɠallamúuna fii haadíhi lmadaarísi
llaylíiyah(-ti) / taśjíiɠan láhum. / fa jtámaɠa lfallaaħúuna ħáwlah(u)
/ wa dáɠa lmufattíśu mr@@?atan mínhum / w@ T@laba mínhaa ?an
t@qr@?a kalimátan ?aśó@@r@ ?iláyhaa fii kitáab(in) [/] káana fii
yádih(i). / f@ q@r@?at bi S@wtin ɠáal(in): / 'mindíil(un)'. / f@
q@@la láhaa: / '?aħsánt(i)' / wa ?aɠT@@haa mindíilaa. / tumma

dáɡaa r@julan w@ T@laba mính(u) [/] ?an y@qr@?a kalimátan
?aʃ@@r@ ?iláyhaa / f@ q@r@?a bi súrɡah(-tin): / 'táwr(un)'. / wa
káanati lkalimátu ʃáy?an ?@@x@r(@). / f@ q@@la láhu lmufát-
tiʃ(u): / '?únƉur jayyídan w@ qr@?!' / fa n@Ɖ@r@ rr@julu
m@rr@tan ?úxr@@ w@ q@@l(a): / 'táwr(un)'. / f@ q@@mat zawjátuhu w@ q@@lat: / 'záwjii yuħsínu lqir@@?ah(-ta) / walaakinnáhu
fii ħaajátin ʃadiidátin ?ilaa táwrin yaħrútu bíhi l?@rD(@)'. /

'A society has been formed in one of the towns / whose object is to
combat illiteracy. / This society has opened [/] night-schools in the
villages and towns / to teach peasants and artisans [/] reading and
writing. / One day it sent an inspector to one of the villages / carrying
gifts for those learning in these night-schools / as an encouragement
to them. / The peasants gathered round him / and the inspector
called a woman from among them / and asked her to read a word
which he pointed at in a book [/] (which was) in his hand. / And she
read in a loud voice: / 'Kerchief'. / He said to her: / 'Well done!' /
and gave her a kerchief. / Then he called a man and asked him [/] to
read a word he pointed at. / He hastily read out: / 'Ox!' / but the
word was something else. / The inspector said to him: / 'Look
carefully and (then) read!' / And the man looked a second time and
said: / 'Ox!' / Then his wife stood up and said: / 'My husband reads
well / but greatly needs an ox with which to plough the land.' /

Note

Comments on certain features of accentuation in the above passage are
made in the following chapter.

7

ACCENTUATION

7.1 General

Reference was earlier made to the availability to educated speakers of more than one Classical pronunciation (p. 77). The measures of morphology and syntax will, of course, at once reveal whether the language used is Classical or a variety of spoken language which includes vernacular forms. In general, from a phonetic standpoint, the degree of divergence from vernacular practice may be used to assess the 'grade' of Classical pronunciation—the greater the divergence, the more Classical the performance. Public address, for example, especially of a non-political kind, will be 'more Classical' than the reading aloud of a newspaper article, and the latter style will reveal greater or less 'vernacular influence' in response to the degree of education of any listener. The basis of pronunciation differences is not, however, solely stylistic but importantly also regional. Arabs of every Arab country, and even of districts within them, have their own idea of how, for instance, certain consonants should be pronounced, yet different pronunciations, if used systematically, may still be used without invalidating the description 'Classical' as applied to the rendering of a given text. The fact that the Libyan, for example, does not distinguish between Ð and D does not render his 'Classical' vernacular, nor is the same text any less Classical for being spoken by an Egyptian with his notably different speech habits. The Egyptian simply enjoys the advantage of a norm regularly provided by or derivable from the usage of the 'Ulamā'[1] 'scholars' of Al-Azhar and Dār al-'Ulūm, the teachers' training college in Cairo. Certain forms of Classical Arabic, generally perceived as 'high Classical', for example the reading of the Quran and of classical poetry, require highly specialized techniques, maintained by tradition and specialist schools of the kind just mentioned. The 'languages' of the Quran and the newspaper, though sharing most of their grammar, differ markedly not only

---

[1] In our transcription, ǧulamáa?.

from a lexical but also from a phonetic point of view. It has been made clear that the study of Quranic reading, recitation and chant does not lie within the scope of this book.

'Vernacular influence' is nowhere more clearly in evidence than in the matter of accentuation. The facts as stated below are the outcome of research with Egyptians of academic standing, but are at variance with the 'rules' propounded in some grammars of Classical Arabic,[1] in which, for example, the instruction to accent máśw@r@tun 'consultation, deliberation', tajánnabataa 'they (f.) both avoided', mukáatabatun 'correspondence' in the manner indicated conflicts seriously with the regular Egyptian accentuation maśw@r@tun, tajannábataa, mukaatábatun. The facts vary markedly between different parts of the Arab world, but, in view of the inherent interest of the subject, it is surprising to find that the Arab grammarians devote no attention to it.

The syllable which stands out to the ear above the others in the isolated polysyllabic Arabic word may be termed the 'accented' or 'tonic' syllable. Its location derives from the number, quantities and sequence of syllables going to make up the syllabic structure of the whole word. The accented syllable typically carries the strongest stress (or breath force) and the highest pitch. The increase of energy expended on the penultimate syllable and the pitch relationship between all syllables of the English word 'conversátion'—pronounced with typical unemphatic affirmative intonation—corresponds closely in these respects to Arabic yaktubáani 'they (m.) both write', though the unaccented syllables -tu- and -ni of the Arabic form are given greater weight than -ver- and -tion in the English word.

7.2 Syllabic basis of accentuation

It will be remembered that syllables are of the following structural types: CV, CVV, CVC, CVVC, CVCC, CVVCC (see 2.5). These are quantitatively expressed as follows:

Quantity[2]	Structure	Remarks
Short	CV	Consonant+short vowel. Always open.

---

[1] For example, G. W. Thatcher, *Arabic Grammar of the Written Language* (4th edn. London, Lund Humphries, 1942).

[2] It is the combination of syllable quantities that also produces characteristic

Medium   CVV   Consonant+long vowel or consonant+short
           CVC   vowel+consonant, thus both open and closed.
Long   CVVC   Always closed. CVVC can only occur non-final
           CVCC   if the second consonant is part of a geminate
           CVVCC   cluster. CVCC and CVVCC can only occur
                    final. CVVCC, relatively rare, must contain a
                    final geminate cluster.

Accentuation is a function of the combination of these structures, of which a representative selection follows. The examples are all unsuffixed, but suffixed forms, as will appear later, do not modify but simply extend the basis of the rules on which accentuation rests. Particle prefixes, including the article, though in some cases fused with the word in Arabic writing, play no part in accentuation.[1] The word in isolation may be pronounced in two forms, pausal and non-pausal, for example in the context of teaching, and examples of both are included. The terms *oxytone*, *paroxytone* and *proparoxytone* respectively refer to an accented ultimate, penultimate and ante-penultimate syllable:

Word	Syllabic structure	Accentual type
D@r@bt 'I/you (s.m.) struck'	CV-CV́CC	Oxytone
?a9máal 'acts, actions'	CVC-CV́VC	Oxytone
ḥaajjáat 'having confuted (f.pl.); having made the pilgrimage to Mecca (f.pl.)'	CVVC-CV́VC	Oxytone
yuS@llúun 'they (m.) pray'	CV-CVC-CV́VC	Oxytone
yursiláan 'they (m.) both send'	CVC-CV-CV́VC	Oxytone
muśtaaq@@t 'yearning (f.pl.); yearnings'	CVC-CVV-CV́VC	Oxytone
m@@rr@táan 'two passers-by (f.)'	CVVC-CV-CV́VC	Oxytone
yataḥaddáwn 'they (m.) compete'	CV-CV-CVC-CV́CC	Oxytone
?áḥad 'one'	CV́-CVC	Paroxytone
qúmtum 'you (pl.m.) rose'	CV́C-CVC	Paroxytone
śáadda 'he argued (with s.o.)'	CV́VC-CV	Paroxytone
katábtum 'you (pl.m.) wrote'	CV-CV́C-CVC	Paroxytone
mustáśfaa 'hospital'	CVC-CV́C-CVV	Paroxytone

Arabic rhythms. Each syllable must be accorded its due quantitative measure or 'rhythmic weight'.

   [1] This is not true of certain regional varieties of vernacular Arabic outside Egypt.

Word	Syllabic structure	Accentual type
haadáani 'these (m.) two' (nominative)	CVV-CV́V-CV	Paroxytone
śaabbáatun 'young women'	CVVC-CV́V-CVC	Paroxytone
yataq@@talúuna 'they (m.) fight with one another'	CV-CV-CVV-CV-CV́V-CV	Paroxytone
mutahakkimúuna 'they (m.) have passed judgment'	CV-CV-CVC-CV-CV́V-CV	Paroxytone
mušt@qq@táani 'two derivatives'	CVC-CVC-CV-CV́V-CV	Paroxytone
q@ttála 'he killed, massacred'	CVC-CV́-CV	Paroxytone
q@ttálat 'she killed, massacred'	CVC-CV́-CVC	Paroxytone
kaatába 'he corresponded'	CVV-CV́-CV	Paroxytone
kaatábaa 'they (m.) both corresponded'	CVV-CV́-CVV	Paroxytone
m@@rr@tun 'passer-by (f.)'	CVVC-CV́-CVC	Paroxytone
mugallímun 'teacher (m.)'	CV-CVC-CV́-CVC	Paroxytone
katabtúmaa 'you (m. and f.) both wrote'	CV-CVC-CV́-CVV	Paroxytone
must@qbílun 'radio receiver'	CVC-CVC-CV́-CVC	Paroxytone
muhm@@rr@tun 'blushing, having turned red (s.f.)'	CVC-CVVC-CV́-CVC	Paroxytone
kátaba 'he wrote'	CV́-CV-CV	Proparoxytone
kátabaa 'they (m.) both wrote'	CV́-CV-CVV	Proparoxytone
?inkás@r@ 'it (m.) got broken'	CVC-CV́-CV-CV	Proparoxytone
kaatábataa 'they (f.) both corresponded'	CVV-CV́-CV-CVV	Proparoxytone
w@@qífatun[1] 'standing still (s.f.)'	CVV-CV́-CV-CVC	Proparoxytone
bulahníyatun 'abundance, wealth'	CV-CVC-CV́-CV-CVC	Proparoxytone
muq@@tílatun 'combatants'	CV-CVV-CV́-CV-CVC	Proparoxytone
mutajanníbatun 'avoiding (s.f.)'	CV-CV-CVC-CV́-CV-CVC	Proparoxytone
kalimátun 'word'	CV-CV-CV́-CVC	Paroxytone
katabátaa 'they (f.) both wrote'	CV-CV-CV́-CVV	Paroxytone
murtabiT@tun 'linked with; bound by (s.f.)'	CVC-CV-CV-CV́-CVC	Paroxytone

[1] @@ is somewhat fronted here, with i in the following syllable.

Comparison between pausal and non-pausal forms at once reveals the link between syllable pattern and accentuation. For example, different specific syllables of the same word muɡallim(un) 'teacher' are accented in its pausal form muɡállim and non-pausal form muɡallímun. From an accentual point of view, muɡállim is classifiable with, say, mustáʂfaa 'hospital'. There is no 'shift' of accent between muɡállim and muɡallímun; the trisyllabic muɡállim and tetrasyllabic muɡallímun are simply examples of different syllabic structures within which accentual incidence is fixed. From a reading point of view, it is, of course, necessary for the reader to decide in advance where he will locate his pauses; if muɡallímun is to be treated as a pausal form, then not only must -un be omitted but the accent must fall on -ɡal, whereas if -un is included, then the syllable -li- is to be accented. The accentual difference is entailed by pause as opposed to non-pause and is not properly spoken of as accentual 'shift'.[1] Similarly, one should not regard as 'inherently' accented the first syllables of, say, pausal kátab 'he wrote' and non-pausal kátaba. The two forms are again differently classifiable, kátab with e.g. ʔáħad 'one' and kátaba with e.g. ʔinkás@r@ 'it got broken'.

7.3 Detailed analysis

Examination of the examples shows that all forms which contain an ultimate long syllable are oxytonic, e.g. D@r@bt, ʔaɡmáal, yuS@llúun, etc., whereas those forms whose ultimate is not long are variously paroxytonic and proparoxytonic, e.g. kaatába but kátaba, katabátaa but kátabaa. The first major division, therefore, is into long-ultimate (L) and not-long ultimate (Ƚ). As far as disyllables are concerned, this division is definitive, i.e. once the structure of the ultimate syllable is known, there is no need to subdivide the penultimate as to its structure, cf. r@ʔaa 'he saw', q@@lat 'she said', qúmtum 'you (pl.m.) rose', ʂáadda 'he argued'. In longer forms whose ultimate syllable is not-long, it is necessary to distinguish in pre-ultimate places between short CV and all other syllable quantities, i.e. short (S) and not-short (Ƨ). Thus, the earlier system of three quantities, short/medium/long, is not relevant to

---

[1] Accentual 'shift' does occur in English. Cf., for example, 'I said "Hámitic" [elsewhere 'Hamític'], not "Sémitic" [elsewhere 'Semític']'.

accentuation in the way that might have been expected, though it is, of course, of very great importance to the proper *rhythmic* pronunciation of Arabic based on the quantitative differentiation of syllables. In the formulation of accentual rules a twofold distinction suffices between S and Ş, L and Ł, with respective reference to pre-ultimate and ultimate syllables. Medium quantity CVV and CVC are not-short in pre-ultimate syllables and not-long in ultimate syllables. CV is short in pre-ultimate syllables and not-long in ultimate syllables, whereas CVVC is not-short in pre-ultimate syllables and CVVC/CVCC/CVVCC are long in ultimate syllables. It will be appreciated how, in spite of some superficial resemblance, the basis of accentuation in Arabic differs greatly from that in English. The place of the English accent is mostly unpredictable, cf. íssue/ensúe, végetable/divísible, labóratory/nationálity, édible/eléven, ópposite/fanátic, abóminable/aboríginal, inéligible/illegítimate, and so on. Series of the type pólitics/polítical/politícian, télephone/telephónic/teléphonist, etc., show, too, how vowel quality in English varies with accentual incidence, and the student of Arabic must remember how important it is to avoid this vocalic variation in Arabic and also to give short unaccented Arabic syllables their full weight, in contrast with the fact of their reduction in English often to the point of elimination, as in, say, 'p(o)líce', 'univérs(i)ty', etc. As to Arabic, the fact that accentuation is part of the total syllable pattern of a word is fundamentally more interesting than that it is necessary, in order to account for it, to recognize such abstract categories as C and V, L and Ł, S and Ş.

The great majority of CA words, of which pronominal suffixes may form part, are paroxytonic, and even oxytones are usually pausal forms which correspond to paroxytonic non-pausal counterparts. It is only such forms as (non-pausal) kátaba, (non-pausal) ?inkás@r@ or kaatábataa that are neither oxytonic nor paroxytonic but regularly proparoxytonic. There is thus variation between paroxytones and proparoxytones among words whose ultimate and penultimate syllables are respectively not-long and short, e.g. kaatába but kátaba, katabátaa but kaatábataa. This accentual difference is, in fact, accounted for by the quantitative difference S:Ş between *preceding* syllables, i.e. ka- (S) in kátaba or (kátabaa) and kaa- (Ş) in kaatába (or kaatábaa), and again, between ka- (S) in katabátaa and kaa- (Ş) in kaatábataa. Once the principle of the influence of antepenultimate and earlier syllables is recognized, analytical simplification is achieved by positing a zero post-pausal syllable (#) and equating it with $, so that e.g. #kátaba is of a quantitative piece with ?inkás@r@. The equipollence of # and $ applies throughout, for example in the following pairs of forms:

| # | r@?aa | } paroxytonic |
| kaa | tábaa | |

| # | kátaba | } proparoxytonic |
| ?in | kás@r@ | |

| # | śaj@r@tun | } paroxytonic |
| ?ad | wiyatúhu | |

| # | b@q@r@tuhaa | } proparoxytonic |
| ?ad | wiyatúhumaa | |

The longest sequence of S-syllables seems to be illustrated by b@q@r@tuhúmaa '(dual) their cow', paroxytonic in contrast with proparoxytonic ?adwiyatúhumaa '(dual) their medicine'.

In brief, therefore, in order to locate the accent, the following steps are necessary:

(1) start from the end of the word;

(2) if the ultimate syllable is long (CVVC, CVCC, CVVCC), it is accented;

(3) if the ultimate syllable is not-long (CV, CVV, CVC) and the penultimate is not-short (CVV, CVC, CVVC), then the penultimate is accented;

(4) if the ultimate is not-long and the penultimate is short (CV), then variously the penultimate or antepenultimate is accented in accordance with the quantity of the antepenultimate, pre-antepenultimate or earlier syllables, including zero. Accentual incidence under (4) may be specified in tabular form as follows:

$ or #/S/Ł	Paroxytonic	kaatába, q@ttálat, maktábah, m@@rr@tun 'passer-by (f.)'; r@?aa, kátab, híya
$ or #/S/S/Ł	Proparoxytonic	?inkás@r@, kaatábataa, bulahníyatun; kátaba, kátabaa, śáj@r@h
$ or #/S/S/S/Ł	Paroxytonic	?adwiyatúhu, murtabiT@tun; śaj@r@tun, katabátaa

Ś or ♯/S/S/S/S/Ł Proparoxytonic   ?adwiyatúhumaa;

śaj@r@tuhu 'his tree'

S/S/S/S/S/Ł Paroxytonic   śaj@r@tuhúmaa

Notes

1. Clearly, sequences of short syllables are especially relevant to accentuation. Such sequences, rare in vernacular Arabic, are an important characteristic of the Classical language. Sequences of four and five S-syllables occur in suffixed forms, which have been illustrated by those containing the 3 s.m. and 3 dual pronominal suffixes -hu and -humaa.

2. The sequence S/S/S/S/S/Ł of b@q@r@tuhúmaa is characterized by an up-and-down pitch movement in which the first syllable is pitched highest and alternate syllables after the first are pitched higher than those which precede and follow, i.e. ˙ ˙ ˙ ˙ .

3. Although the quantity of even, say, a sixth-last syllable can play its part in the location of the accent, it can only occur on one of the last three syllables. It is of some interest to remark that the Greek-derived terms oxytone, paroxytone and proparoxytone correspond in that order to the use in Spanish today of the terms (*palabra*) *aguda*, *llana* (or *grave*) and *esdrújula*. Similar terms in other romance languages do not nowadays seem to be used as systematically as in Spanish, but cf., for example, Italian (*parola*) *sdrucciola* '(word) with antepenultimate accentuation'.

7.4 Regional difference

The above account of accentuation is based on Egyptian practice, specifically that of Cairo and the Nile Delta. In fact, Classical accentuation reflects vernacular usage in a given region. Paroxytones of the pattern Ś/S/Ł, e.g. maktábah, q@ttálat, etc., are seized upon by speakers from other parts of the Arab world as characteristically Egyptian. In the Levant, for example, the pattern regularly produces proparoxytones, and that the difference is felt to be striking is doubtless due to the statistical frequency of the pattern. Such differences do not, of course, prejudice intelligibility, and, in any case, practice in the regions is preponderantly similar. The fact remains, however, that Classical Arabic, and for that matter also so-called Modern Standard Arabic, is a *Schriftsprache* capable of as much difference of phonetic interpretation between countries as was formerly the ecclesiastical Latin of the Mass. As far as accentuation is concerned, the form katabataa, for instance, is, within a comparatively restricted geographical area, regularly and variously pronounced as (1) an oxytone (Lebanon), (2) a paroxytone (Cairo), (3) a proparoxytone (Levant, e.g. Jordano-Palestinian area), (4) a hypertone[1] (Upper Egypt). Lebanese and Egyptian differences are interesting from several points of view. For example, the Lebanese classicist does not typically distinguish between short and long vowels in post-accentual position, and his r@?a, háwwa 'he ventilated', r@q@bati 'my neck' will correspond to the Azhari-trained Egyptian's r@?aa, háwwaa, r@q@bátii. Moreover, the Egyptian kátaba (3 s.m. past tense) and kátabaa (3 dual past), i.e. both proparoxytonic and distinguished by a difference of vowel length in the ultimate syllable, correspond typically to a Lebanese difference of accentuation as well as ultimate vowel length, i.e. between proparoxytonic kátaba and oxytonic katabáa. Vowel length and accentuation are concomitant in the Lebanese case and serve to mark the dual grammatical category, as also in the corresponding feminine form katabatáa.[2] It will be seen, therefore, that, as far as Lebanon is concerned, in contrast with the Egyptian pronunciation of CA, accentuation has at least in part to be considered within a grammatical framework. Other regular differences of accentuation between Lebanese Classical usage and Egyptian relate to the two patterns we have cited and which are those subject to the greatest amount of regional variation, i.e. S/S/L and S/S/S/L, e.g. máktabah (Egyptian maktábah), mágrifah (Egyptian magrífah), sa?álahu (Egyptian sa?aláhu) 'he asked him', r@q@bati (Egyptian r@q@bátii), mufakkir@tuhu (Egyptian mufakkir@túhu) 'his notebook, diary'. Nor is it necessary to cross national boundaries to find such differences. Although Cairo sets the standard for pronunciation as much for Classical as for vernacular Arabic in Egypt, there nevertheless occur in high Classical pronunciation differences of accentuation attributable to regional contrasts within Egypt. Once again, the two previous patterns are the most noticeable contributing to regional variation between Cairo and the Delta, on the one hand, and Upper Egypt, on the other. Upper Egyptians trained in classical orthoepy

---

[1] The term is invented as a means of referring to those forms whose accentuation 'goes (back) beyond' the antepenultimate syllable.

[2] The dual category is not the only one involved. A. F. L. Beeston has pointed out that Khalil Semaan (? of Lebanese background) refers on p. 37 of his *Linguistics in the Middle Ages* (Leiden, 1968) to the pausal form of the accusative termination -an as 'a stressed [*sic*] long vowel /ā/'.

modify their word-forms in the context of isolated words, but in connected speech their vernacular usage often influences their treatment of the two patterns in question. These are illustrated by wajadataa 'they (dual f.) found' and qiT9ata 'piece, morsel' (accusative) in the first line of the well-known fable beginning hirr@taani wajadataa qiT9ata jubn 'Two cats found a piece of cheese'. The Cairene rendering will typically be the expected hirr@táani wajadátaa qiT9áta júbn, i.e. with paroxytonic wajadátaa and qiT9áta, but in the Upper Egyptian reflex hirr@táani wájadataa qíT9ata júbn, hypertonic wájadataa and proparoxytonic qíT9ata occur. It is not surprising to find that in Upper Egyptian vernacular Arabic[1] forms of comparable structure are similarly treated from an accentual standpoint, e.g. 9ágalatak 'your bicycle' and mírwaḥa 'fan'. We shall return in Chapter 8 to consideration of the two patterns, since there may well be a need for further research in relation to their use in connected speech, research that the student may wish to undertake on his own behalf.

7.5 Further practice examples

Here are some additional words of differing syllabic constitution for the purpose of word-practice before we turn to the connected passages of Chapter 8. Pronounce the words in deliberate, measured fashion, carefully maintaining the quantitative difference between syllables irrespective of accentual location. Do not skip over short syllables. If the short syllable is taken as the unit of length, then medium syllables may be taken as $1\frac{1}{2}$ times as long and long syllables as twice as long.

(I) 2-SYLLABLE WORDS (all in pausal form)

Paroxytones	*Oxytones*
húwa 'he'	T@máa9 'greed'
lúǵ@h 'language'	T@bíib 'doctor'
mí?ah 'hundred'	zakáah 'purity'
šákaa 'he complained'	kitáab 'book'
r@maa 'he threw'	murúur 'traffic'
j@r@@ 'it (m.) flowed; it happened'	t@qíil 'heavy (s.m.)'
	?ašádd 'stronger'
q@@maa 'they (m.) both stood up'	maḥáll 'place'

[1] Specifically, that of Qena.

Paroxytones

r@mat 'she threw'
šáaddat 'she argued (with s.o.)'
láysa 'he is not . . . '
xífta 'you (s.m.) feared'
m@r@D 'illness; disease'
ná9am 'yes'
jálas 'he sat down'
?@xD@r 'green (s.m.)'
yáktub 'he writes'
b@rT@l 'he bribed'
máyyit 'dead (s.m.)'
x@bb@r 'he informed'
fíDD@h 'silver'
ħ@@Dir 'ready, prepared'
kúbr@@ 'bigger, older (s.f.)'
?ánsaa 'he made s.o. forget'

Oxytones

mam@rr 'passage; elapsing'
katábt 'I/you (s.) wrote'
da9áwt 'I/you (s.) called'
?aħsánt 'I/you (s.) did well'
?@mT@@r 'rains'
miqd@@r 'amount'
miSríiy 'Egyptian; Cairene'
tadxíin 'smoking'
mawjúud 'present; existent (s.m.)'
finjáan 'cup'
malláaħ 'sailor'
?aššáam 'Syria; Damascus'
kuttáab 'Quranic school'
bur9úut 'flea'
?aaláa? 'blessings, benefits'
?aab@@r 'wells'
ħiiT@@n 'walls'
m@@rr@@t 'passers-by (pl.f.)'

(II) 3-SYLLABLE WORDS (non-pausal forms marked *)

Paroxytones

katábnaa 'we wrote'
katábtu* 'I wrote'
?am@rtuh 'I ordered him'
r@dádna 'they (f.) returned (s.t.)'
r@dádnaa 'we returned (s.t.)'
muhándis 'engineer'
mufáttiš 'inspector'
tasállam 'he received'
?istá?j@r 'he rented'
?istád9aa 'he summoned'
kuntúnna 'you (pl.f.) were'
?iħm@rruu 'they turned red'
mawáaddun* 'substance, material'
safíinah 'ship'
tajáarib 'experiments'
ŧiyáabuh 'his clothes'
kitáabii 'my book'
ħukúumah 'government'
muSíibah 'misfortune, calamity'
S@ħ@@r@@ 'deserts'
duuláabun* 'cupboard'

Oxytones

x@damáat 'services'
tawaríix 'dates; histories'
wuz@r@@? 'ministers'
yadawíiy 'manual (s.m.)'
wajadúuh 'they found it (m.)'
duwalíiy 'international (s.m.)'
mafaatíiš 'keys'
sif@@r@@t 'embassies'
ru?asáa? 'chairmen; heads'
mudiirúun 'directors'
q@liilúun 'few'
xuSuuSíiy 'private (s.m.)'
sulaymáan 'Solomon'
maħ@TT@@t 'stations'
?aħibbáa? 'friends, loved ones'
?istiláam 'receiving'
turjumáan 'guide, interpreter'
?ummaháat 'mothers'
?@9niyáa? 'rich (pl.), rich men'
sayyidáat 'ladies'
waajibáat 'duties'

Paroxytones

ʔuuláaʔik 'those'
ʔalbáariħ 'yesterday'
sayy@@r@h 'car'
ʔ@9Tíini 'give me!'
9@@Símah 'capital (city)'
kaanátaa 'they (f.) both were'
jaahílaa 'ignorant (s.m.
    accusative)'
q@l9átun* 'fort'
madr@sah 'school'
ʔimr@ʔah 'woman'
q@ttálat 'she killed'
ʔ@ħSínah 'horses'
baytúhu* 'his house'
ʔinházam 'he was defeated'
yaħtárim 'he respects'
ʔuktúbaa 'both of you write!'
m@@rr@tun* 'passer-by,
    pedestrian (f.)'

Oxytones

haaʔuláaʔ 'these, those'
sayy@@r@@t 'cars'
T@bb@@xúun 'cooks'
kubbaayáat 'glasses, tumblers'
m@wDuu9áat 'subjects, topics'
n@Sr@@níiy 'Christian'
ʔistisláam 'surrender'
ʔalx@rTúum 'Khartoum'
ʔiħt@r@mt 'I/you (s.) respected'
ʔiħm@r@rt 'I/you (s.) blushed'
ʔistaħ@qq 'he deserved'
musta9ídd 'ready, prepared (for
    s.t.)'
lisaanáyn 'two tongues' (oblique)
tasallámt 'I/you (s.) received'
tajaahált 'I/you (s.) feigned
    ignorance'
ʔista9lámt 'I/you (s.) inquired'

Proparoxytones

fátaħa* 'he opened'
w@r@q@h 'sheet of paper, leaf'
kátabat 'she wrote'
s@r@q@h 'thieves'
kálimah 'word'
xúT@bun* 'sermons'
júbunun* 'foreheads'
wáladuh 'his son'
tám@ruh 'its (m.) fruit'
w@S@luu 'they arrived'
w@S@laa 'they both arrived'

(III) 4-SYLLABLE WORDS

Paroxytones

mutaw@ssiT 'middle, median'
mutanáffas 'breathing-space'
yataħáddaa 'he competes with'
yatabáaħat 'he discusses with'
yadawíiyah 'manual (s.f.)'
wuz@r@@ʔu* 'ministers'
ʔid@@r@tun* 'management'

Oxytones

mu9allimúun 'teachers (m.)'
mußtarikúun 'participants (m.)'
ħayawaanáat 'animals'
ʔijtimaa9áat 'meetings'
ʔimtiħaanáat 'examinations'
T@wiilatáan 'long (dual f.)'
f@r@nsaawíiy 'French'

Paroxytones

ŧalaaŧátun* 'three'
yaktubúuna* 'they (m.) write'
ʔiħm@r@rnaa 'we reddened'
fataħtúnna 'you (pl.f.) opened'
ʔistaħsánta* 'you (s.m.) approved of'
ʔistayq@Ðnaa 'we woke up'
ʔistaɣáadat 'she recalled, called back'
masaajíinu* 'prisoners'
śay@@Tíinu* 'devils'
D@r@búuhaa 'they hit her'
tadulláani* 'they (f.) both show'
naaʔimáani* 'asleep (dual m.)'
mulaaq@@tun* 'meeting, encounter'
fallaaħúuna* 'peasants'
muśtaaq@@tun* 'yearning (pl.f.)'
bunduqíiyah 'rifle'
yuunaaníiyah 'Greek language'
malikátun* 'queen'
w@S@látaa 'they (f.) both arrived'
fataħáhu* 'he opened it (m.)'
talaamíðah 'scholars, pupils'
ħukuumátun* 'government'
kawaakíbu* 'stars'
muSiibátun* 'calamity, misfortune'
mufattíśun* 'inspector'
ʔixwaanúhum 'their (m.) brothers, colleagues'
zaytuunátun* 'an olive'
ta?@xx@r@t 'she was late'
taħaadáŧat 'she conversed with'
ħasabtúhu* 'I considered him (to be . . .)'
D@r@bánii 'he hit me'
must@qbálun* 'future'
muħm@@rr@tun* 'reddening, reddened (s.f.)'
talajlájat 'she stammered'

Oxytones

sulaamiiyáat 'bones' (of hand or foot)
musta9m@r@@t 'colonies'

Proparoxytones

ʔitt@x@ða* 'he adopted, took s.t. on'
ʔiltája?a* 'he took refuge'
ʔinkás@r@t 'it (f.) broke (intrans.)'
tarbíyatuh 'his upbringing, education'
kaatábataa 'the two of them (f.) corresponded'
ǵ@@yátuhaa 'her intention'
w@@qífatun* 'standing still (s.f.)'
madr@satun* 'school'
muśkílatun* 'problem, difficulty'

The longer the pattern, the fewer the examples and the greater the appeal that has to be made to non-pausal forms and pronominal suffixation. The maximum number of syllables appears to be seven, and a hypothetical form like *?ittif@@qiiyaatuhumaa will be 'replaced' by such a phrasal element as ?ittif@@qiiyáatun baynáhumaa 'agreements between the two of them', but this, too, is an area where further research is needed and which the learner can himself explore with the help of the Arabic speaker. 5-syllable words are quite common, and there follow some examples of 5-, 6- and 7-syllables. It would be unrealistic to extend forms beyond this limit, for example by means of pronominal suffixes, and as in the hypothetical 8-syllable form given above, and, indeed, even below the limit, some disagreement must be expected over the acceptability of this or that item. Any such disagreement would belong to areas of variability and flexibility that are, after all, built into any language, including one so rigidly codified as Classical Arabic.

(IV) 5-SYLLABLE WORDS

Paroxytones

wajadtumúunii 'you (pl.m.) found me'

muɡallimúuya 'my teachers'

yastaḥsinúuna* 'they (m.) appreciate, admire'

muśtaaq@táani* 'yearning (dual f.)'

mukaatibáatun* 'reporters (pl.f.)'

yaktatibúuna* 'they (m.) make a copy of'

mustaḥiṭṭúuna* 'urging, prompting (pl.m.)'

?aśśariiɡátu* 'the Sharia or Islamic law'

wuz@r@@?úhum 'their ministers'

mustafiiD@tun* 'elaborate, exhaustive (s.f.)'

murtabiT@tun* 'connected, linked (s.f.)'

must@qillátun* 'independent (s.f.)'

Oxytones

?ittif@@qiiyáat 'agreements'

yataq@@talúun 'they fight with one another'

mutaq@@tiláat 'fighting (pl.f.) with one another'

mutasallimúun 'receiving, having received (pl.m.)'

munaafisatáan '(two) contestants (f.)'

Proparoxytones

bulahníyatun* 'wealth, abundance'

r@faahíyatun* 'luxuries'

bay@@Tír@tun* 'veterinary surgeons'

malaa?íkatun* 'angels'

mukaatábatun* 'correspondence'

mustaɡm@r@tun* 'colony'

(v) 6-SYLLABLE WORDS

Paroxytones

yataq@@talúuna* 'they (m.) fight with one another'

munaafisatáani* 'two contestants (f.)'

mutajannibáatun* 'keeping away from (pl.f.)'

mutahakkimúuna* 'having their (pl.m) own way'

?al?iskandaríiyah 'Alexandria'

?alqusT@nTiiníiyah 'Constantinople, Istanbul'

Proparoxytones

mutajanníbatun* 'keeping away from (s.f.)'

mutaq@@tílatun* 'fighting with (s.f.)'

(VI) 7-SYLLABLE WORDS

Paroxytones

mutanaafisatáani* 'rivals (dual f.)'

mutajannibatáani* 'keeping away from (dual f.)'.

It is also good learning practice to collect series of related forms and to compare them from the point of view of accentuation. Take, for example, pausal and non-pausal forms, e.g. dáalik/ daalíka* 'that (s.m.)', q@@til/q@@tílun* 'killer', murtábiT@h/ murtabiT@tun* 'connected, linked (s.f.)', etc., or compare unsuffixed and (variously) suffixed forms, e.g. majállah/majalláat 'magazine/magazines', šáj@r@h 'tree'/šaj@r@@t '(some) trees'/ šaj@r@tuhaa 'her tree'/šaj@r@tuhúmaa 'their (dual) tree', kátaba* 'he wrote'/katábna 'they (f.) wrote'/kaatábaa 'they (dual m.) corresponded', etc. Here are a few further paired examples of unsuffixed and suffixed forms, which at the same time may be used for additional practice in the 'quantitative' reading of Arabic words:

Unsuffixed	Suffixed
r@mat	r@máthu* 'she threw it (m.)'
?áhad	?ahadúhum 'one of them (m.)'
šáadda*	šaaddáhu* 'he argued with him'
?@rD@@	?@rD@@hu* 'he pleased him'
katábti*	katabtíhi* 'you (s.f.) wrote it (m.)'
q@ttálat	q@ttaláthum 'she caused carnage among them (m.)'
?istálq@@	?istalq@@hu* 'he threw him down'
mustášfaa	mustašfáahaa 'her hospital'
kaatábaa	kaatabáahu* 'they (m.) both corresponded with him'

Unsuffixed	*Suffixed*
katabátaa	katabatáahu* 'they (f.) both wrote it (m.)'
kaatábataa	kaatabatáahu* 'they (f.) both corresponded with him'
yatabáahat	yatabaaháthaa 'he discusses it (f.) with'
?@Sdiq@@?u*	?@Sdiq@@?úhu* 'his friends'
yuhaddiṭáani*	yuhaddiṭaaníhi* 'they (m.) both relate it (m.)'
yadulláani*	yadullaaníhi* 'they (m.) both show it (m.)'
muhaddiṭúun	muhaddiṭuuhúmaa 'telling (pl.m.) the two of them'
musaaɣadáatun*	musaaɣadaatúhu* 'his encouragements'
samaaɣiiyáatun*	samaaɣiiyaatúhu* 'its (m.) acoustics'
ɣaaʃuur@@?u*	ɣaaʃuur@@?úhu* 'his Ashūra' (feast)
?adwíyatun*	?adwiyatúhu* 'his medicine'
?aɣmáalun*	?aɣmaalúhumaa 'their (dual m.) actions'
q@@máatun*	q@@maatúhumaa 'their (dual m.) statures'
q@ttála*	q@ttálahum 'he massacred them (m.)'
must@nSir	must@nSíruhu* 'asking (s.m.) him for help'
kaatába*	kaatábahu* 'he corresponded with him'
hijjáatun*	hijjaatúhumaa 'the pilgrimages of the two of them'
hásanun*	hasanúhumaa 'the nice one of the two (m.)'.

8

THE RHYTHMS AND INTONATION
OF READING ALOUD

8.1 General

In earlier chapters, with the main exception of Chapter 6, concern
has been with words. In this chapter, emphasis is on the phrase and
similar stretches as well as sentences and longer elements. Illustra-
tions are provided from passages in *Writing Arabic* which are
reproduced in Appendix A. Proceeding slowly at first helps the
learner to avoid infelicitous stops and starts, hesitations, hummings
and hawings, and to inculcate in himself the confidence necessary to
speak out at all times positively and vigorously in the Arab manner.
Words and phrases should first be practised before they are run
together into breath- and sense-groups.

It is quite un-Arabic to pause on and unwantedly lengthen a
vowel which is omissible pre-pausally. Such vowels are better
dropped altogether than brought into undesirable prominence.
Again, if pause is advertently made before hamzátu lw@Sl (6.2), for
example in the case of the article, it has to be remembered to
include the glottal stop before proceeding, but, better still, pause in
such places should be avoided. It is important, therefore, to decide
beforehand where pauses will be made.

Once words and phrases have been fully and satisfactorily rehearsed, then passages should be taken sentence by sentence. Much
practice will be necessary, involving considerable repetition. Passages should be learned and memorized, so that there is no longer
any need to read them. Most practice will have to be undertaken in
private, but in the class-room, under the teacher's guidance, the
learner should repeat the material word by word, phrase by phrase,
sentence by sentence, going over it again and again, revising it with
the teacher and insisting on meticulous correction, until 'perfec-
tion' is achieved. In the early stages, too much should not be
attempted. The beginner cannot expect to read Arabic, even in
roman form, in the fluent way in which he reads his own or other

more familiar languages. There is the world of difference, too, between silent reading and reading aloud.

One passage should be perfected before the next is attempted. Remarkably few passages are needed in order to exhaust the phonetic possibilities. It is also important to seize as many opportunities as offer themselves for training the ear to Arabic utterance. Dictation of words, phrases, sentences and extended passages is highly beneficial, and the teacher should make frequent use of it, until pupils' errors have become exceptional. The more conjoint exercise of the eye, the articulatory musculature and the monitoring ear, the better. The final stages, of course, will be the reading aloud of the text in Arabic script, first vowelled, then unvowelled.

8.2 Quantity and rhythm

Stress has already been placed on the importance of giving Arabic syllables their due weight. Long syllables (CVVC(C), CVCC), except in the rare case of gemination following a long vowel, occur only pre-pausally, so that continuous speech is mostly made up of short (CV) and medium (CVV, CVC) syllables, between which the quantitative difference must be maintained. The long vowel of CVV is quite often lengthened to exceed the 2 × V measure spoken of earlier, perhaps especially in the case of the long *open* vowel, as in the first article of the Muslim creed (?aśhádu ?al (< ?an)) láa ?iláaha ?íll@ ll@@h '(I believe that) there is no god but God'. Getting the accents and pitches (8.3) right, and at the same time dwelling on the long vowels without unacceptably reducing their short counterparts, imparts to the spoken text that dignified, measured sonorousness that is characteristic of Classical reading and recitation. In fact, Quranic recitation proper recognizes more degrees of vowel length than those we have specified. In particular, the long open vowel preceding ? or gemination receives a noticeable increment of length, which in turn varies contextually as to extent. It is least before ? initial in the following word (láa ?áktub 'I shall not write') and greatest before pre-pausal gemination (m@@rr 'passer-by, pedestrian'). Between the two come the vowel preceding ? in the same word (jáa?a 'he came') and that preceding a non-pausal geminate (m@@rrun), the latter longer than the former. But these features belong to Quranic recitation and are not our concern, for which it suffices to recall that a long vowel may in general, though especially in the case of long fátḥah, be somewhat lengthened without offence in both non-pausal and particularly pre-pausal position.

It is important not to pause after a word-final CV syllable, since the syllable will then be interpreted as CVV and rhythm and sense possibly lost. For example, one should not pause on -fa of ḥádafa in the sentence fa ḥádafa kalimáta 'yubáaɢ' 'And he removed the word "Sold"' (from 'The Fishmonger's Sign' in Appendix A). Not only would it be nonsensical to imply a dual interpretation for the verb, but the transition -fa ka- must be performed smoothly in a manner appropriate to the syllabification of the text. Again, if a pause is made after -ta of kalimáta—as it may be for 'dramatic' effect—then it should not be excessive, and the vowel must on no account be lengthened. As helpfully happens, intonational features (8.3) correlate remarkably closely with word and phrase divisions, yet it is still necessary to observe the relative rhythmic quantities of the syllables. The junctions of words, therefore, must be practised in this sense, beyond the features spoken of in Chapter 6.

The text just cited—fa ḥádafa kalimáta 'yubáaɢ'—illustrates a succession of CV syllables. There must be no reduction of any of them in the English manner, especially therefore of the unaccented ones, and at the same time care must be taken not to lengthen any of the consonants, especially following an accented vowel. The syllables should be split up at first, i.e. fa-ḥá-da-fa-ka-li-má-ta . . . , and practice thereafter should build up to a natural tempo, without pause till after -ta, if even then.

In contrast with the preceding text, the phrase li taɢlíimi lfallaaḥíina wa lɢummáal 'for the teaching of peasants and artisans' (from 'The Rewards of Reading' at the end of this chapter) comprises chiefly medium syllables together with two short and the frequently pre-pausal long, i.e. li-taɢ-líi-mil-fal-laa-ḥíi-na-wal-ɢum-máal. These medium syllables should not be hurried over but pronounced in a deliberate, carefully measured style. A small increment of length given to a long vowel will usually not offend. Again, pauses between words must be avoided.

The following clause from the same passage illustrates the most frequent pattern, namely, the admixture of short and medium syllables: wa káanati lkalimátu šáy?an ?@@x@r 'and the word was something else'. Once again, inter-word pauses are to be avoided and the text split up as follows: wa-káa-na-til-ka-li-má-tu-šáy-?an-

?@@-x@r. Further examples of admixture from the passages in Appendix A, section 2, and at the end of this chapter are: min-?á-ḥa-di-ṣa-baa-bíi-ki-d@@-rih (min ?áḥadi ṣabaabíiki d@@rih) 'from one of the windows of his house', wa-láa-ya-záa-lut-taḥ-qíi-qu-mus-ta-mír-r@n (wa láa yazáalu ttaḥqíiqu mustamírr@n) 'and the investigation is still continuing', ?u-ríi-du-?an-?u-saa-wí-ya-hu-bil-?@S-ǵ@r (?uríidu ?an ?usaawíyahu bi l?@Sǵ@r) 'I want to make it the same size as the smaller one', and the learner may add his own.

8.3 Intonation

It should be said again that concern here is with features of voice-pitch in the normal narrative style of reading aloud, that is, neither with Quranic recitation and chant nor with everyday conversation. The salient features to which attention is drawn are nevertheless shared with the vernacular language.

It will be necessary to train the ear to perceive the pitch differences to which reference will be made, and a notation will be supplied to help meet this objective. For initial purposes, differences of pitch may be practised on a single syllable—say, laa—within the limits of an imaginary musical stave (‾‾). A basic twofold distinction is to be made between, on the one hand, level or static tone, when the syllable is pronounced on a monotone variously high in the voice range (‾), in the middle (‾) or low (‗), and, on the other hand, moving or kinetic tone, during which, by continuous adjustment of the vocal cords, pitch falls, either from a low onset (⟍) or a high one (⟍), or falls and rises on the same syllable (⟍⟋). The reader may be surprised to see no mention of a corresponding continuously rising tone, but, in contrast with e.g. Syro-Lebanese Arabic, this does not occur systematically in Egypt, nor for that matter in the neighbouring parts of Libya, though some incidental rise in pitch may accompany what is properly seen as a level tone pitched higher than the preceding syllable or syllables and occurring especially before pause. A relative rise in pitch height occurs between an unaccented and a following accented syllable, but this is not the same thing as a monosyllabic rise, which, in contrast with the fall, is absent from the kind of Arabic that is our subject-matter. The falling–rising tone referred to above involves a fall in pitch over the initial phase of the syllable and a rise over the final phase. As in English, the range of pitch covered by the rising portion is generally less than in the falling phase. It is good practice in the early stages for the teacher to dictate the various tones and ask the student to identify them by number, i.e.

(1)	(2)	(3)	(4)	(5)	(6)
high level	mid level	low level	low fall	high fall	fall-rise

until the response is invariably correct, however much the teacher varies the order of presentation. The student should then be asked to reproduce the tones until he has mastered them in the abstract, so to speak. He may find difficulty in making the fall–rise, though this is an extremely common tone of English. If he does, then he may be asked to reproduce the tone in three parts, ⁻‿⁻ , and then run them together.

There are other pitch refinements which we shall not speak of, since they are irrelevant to the reading style under consideration, but the student can absorb much by listening for the sake of listening to vernacular Arabic with a view to observing not only the rise and fall of the voice but also the use made of, say, voice register (e.g. falsetto versus normal as well as high versus (very) low), any unusual protraction or deceleration/acceleration of syllables, variation in voice quality ('bright', gruff, etc.), and so on, for any language is rich in devices, often of an intonational or associated kind, used for the so-called 'expressive' (e.g. emotive) purposes of language. Let us return, however, to the features that *do* immediately concern us.

As has been said, the rise, occurring on a single syllable and common in English, is not a feature of Egyptian Arabic. In the English interrogative sentence 'Did you get it today?', the lowest intonational point is located, according to rule, on the last accented syllable, i.e. '-day', and a rise typically begins at the onset of the syllable and continues to the end of the sentence.[1] In Egyptian

---

[1] Beyond the introductory stages dealt with in this book, more consideration

pronunciation of hál tasallamtúhu lyáwm?, however, the lowest point is occupied by the syllable -hu l-, whereafter pitch 'jumps' to a higher (sustained) level on the last accented syllable -yawm. It is the difference of pitch between the two syllables that is perceived as constituting the rise, i.e.

        yáwm?

hul

A similar example, in which post-accented syllables are involved, is hál tasallámta risaalátii? 'Did you get my letter?', where there is a jump from the low level of -saa- to the higher level of accented -la- and post-accentual -tii is pronounced on the same pitch as -la-, i.e.

     látii

risaa

Notice that in English, but not in Arabic, the lowest point occurs on the last accent, i.e. le- of 'letter', and the rise takes place between it and the post-accentual final syllable -tter, i.e.

Díd you
      gét my
            tter?
          lé

It may be noted that the rise in these questions is associated typically with the so-called 'Yes/No' type, which may be answered by nágam 'Yes' or laa 'No', in contrast with the type initiated by a specifically interrogative word or particle, e.g. man 'who?', maa 'what?', ?ayy 'which?', mátaa 'when?', limáadaa 'why?', kam 'how much, how many?', which is typically associated with the fall. Exceptions do occur but, once again, they need not detain us.

---

would have to be given to intonational constituency and overall patterns of *sentences*. With special reference to their terminating phases, they are often classified as *tunes*, variously falling, rising, falling–rising, rising–falling, (sustained) level, etc. Analysis in these terms is not undertaken here, though it will be noticed that the closing phases of sentences (or clauses) are typically falling, rising or (sustained) level in reading style. The rising tune is not, of course, the only possible one for the English sentence under reference, but other patterns need not concern us.

It behoves us, before continuing further, to describe the notational conventions used below to indicate intonational form. It is desirable to indicate quantity and accent at the same time as pitch, and this may be done within the stave by marking syllables as follows, with the appropriate mark placed vertically above the vowel of the relevant syllable:

Accented:

(i) level:	short	○
	medium	○
	long	○
(ii) moving (shown on long syllable):	falling	○̦
	falling–rising	○̬
Unaccented:	short	●
	medium	●–●

Thus, the opening sentence of the aforementioned and later fully transcribed fable may be represented:

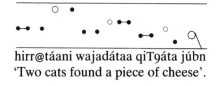

hirr@táani wajadátaa qiT9áta júbn
'Two cats found a piece of cheese'.

The stave is particularly graphic as a mode of representation but it is somewhat cumbersome and certainly space-consuming. To replace it, since the accents and high(er) pitches coincide, it is possible to use the accentual system of acute accents and to extend it to include the grave accent above the vowel of a falling accented syllable, all within the line of writing, i.e. hirr@táani wajadátaa qiT9áta jùbn. In addition, in both modes of representation, a vertical upward arrow may be used to indicate that, as in the foregoing yes/no questions, the following final accent is pronounced, together with any succeeding unaccented syllables, on a higher pitch than the syllables which precede, i.e. hál tasallámta risaa↑látii? The same device, as we shall see later, may be used to indicate the onset of a high fall, again characterized by higher pitch than preceding syllables.

As in English, so in Arabic the accented syllables provide a pattern of intonation for the sentence, and it is largely the behaviour of unaccented syllables that is noticeably different between the two languages. The preceding example is of a straightforward declarative sentence in narrative style, with no word selected for special highlighting by intonational means, as, for example, by a high fall on its last accented syllable or by a fall before the final rhythmic accent followed by sentence-terminating syllables on a low level monotone. The typical pattern is thus one of continuous descent of the 'peaks' provided by the accented syllables, i.e.

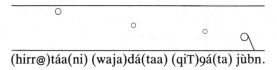

(hirr@)táa(ni) (waja)dá(taa) (qiT)ɡá(ta) jùbn.

The unaccented syllables, however, are in the 'valleys' of the accented 'peaks' (see the full transcription above), whereas in English they typically continue the pattern of descent, as in, say,

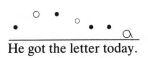

He got the letter today.

The up-and-down pattern of Arabic should not be equated with, for example, Welsh (English) or Hindi/Urdu pronunciation habits, in accordance with which the (stress) accents occur in the valleys and unaccented syllables furnish peaks of pitch prominence, as in e.g.

Cardiff

It is of considerable interest to observe the quite close correlation of pitch accent with words and phrases of the sentence. After the initial 'jump' from the comparatively low to mid level of post-pausal hir-r@- to the first accent on -táa-, the following syllable -ni, which belongs to the same word, maintains the level of -taa- or is pitched only slightly lower. Pitch, however, descends abruptly to wa-ja-before the next jump to -dá-, whereafter the following -taa again maintains the level of -da-, or approximately so. Abrupt descent then occurs again on qiT- before the third jump to -9á-, and thereafter there occurs a further interesting feature. This is that only one post-accentual syllable (-ta) occurs in the word qiT9áta and separates it from the accent of the following word (jùbn). In these circumstances, the post-accentual syllable does not maintain the pitch level of the preceding accent but descends in pitch in order to provide the springboard for the jump to the onset of accented and (final) falling jùbn. There are numerous other examples of this feature in the two passages ('Two Cats and a Monkey' and 'The Rewards of Reading') which are fully transcribed at the end of this chapter. Within the stave and also in the intra-linear transcription (within the line of writing), the descents we have referred to may be indicated by vertical downward arrows, which, though perhaps useful in the early stages, are, strictly speaking, superfluous in view of the word-based regularity with which descent occurs. They would appear as follows:

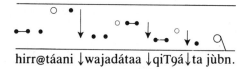

hirr@táani ↓wajadátaa ↓qiT9á↓ta jùbn.

It is also noteworthy that the unaccented syllables in the valleys exhibit their own pattern of descent in parallel with that of the accented syllables. Finally, it should be pointed out that a 'rise' or jump in pitch coincides with an increase of stress or breath-force. The overall effect is not unlike that of scanning the more traditional forms of verse.

So far nothing has been said concerning the falling–rising tone. The fall–rise is infrequent in Arabic, again as opposed to English, where it is often used to mark a contrast of some kind ('Nót hĭm, (but) hèr'). Now and then the tone occurs in similar contrastive use in Arabic, for example in 'The Rewards of Reading' below, where the wife says záwjii yuħsínu lqir@@?ah 'My husband reads well' and continues with walaakinnáhu 'but he . . . '. The implied contrast permits the pre-pausal optional use of the fall–rise on (lqi)r@@?ah, i.e.

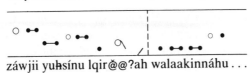

záwjii yuḥsínu lqir@@?ah walaakinnáhu . . .

(The fall–rise is marked ∨ on the accented syllable, which in oxytones carries both the falling and the rising portions of the tone, whereas in other cases the rising portion is carried by post-accentual syllables.) Equally, however, the pre-pausal form may be spoken on a 'suspended' low to mid level tone,[1] i.e.

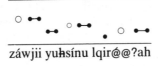

záwjii yuḥsínu lqir@@?ah

as an indication that more is to come—this is, in fact, the general intonational form of pause, with or without any relevance to the possibly contrastive use of a fall–rise, the wholesale importation of which from English into Arabic should be carefully guarded against. In reading, the fall–rise appears predominantly before reported speech, often on an appropriate form of q@@l/y@qúul 'to say'. Examples occur in the specimen passages provided at the end of the chapter.

In principle, and certainly in the reading style of our concern, the accented syllable of the isolated word, suffixed or not, is also accented in the phrase or sentence. In typical unemphatic predication, the last accented syllable bears the fall in declarative sentences and the raised pitch or 'rise' ('jump') in interrogative sentences of the yes/no kind. Verbal, nominal and adverbial elements are as a rule accented—a fact which has the incidental effect of inducing frequent Arab errors in English[2]—whereas particles, nominal and verbal, are rarely accented and are usually treated as of a piece grammatically with the following noun or verb without affecting accentual incidence.[3] Exceptions, however, do occur, for example

---

[1] Marked simply by the acute accent in the intra-linear transcription.

[2] The learner may note that there is usually much to learn on his own account from Arab performance in the learner's language.

[3] This applies not only to, say, prepositional bi or fii but also to e.g. clause-introducing ?an.

with prepositional, interrogative and co-ordinating particles, which may themselves be accented in certain cases when followed by a monosyllabic form, generally itself a further particle, or by the rare pattern CVCV, as in the personal pronouns húwa 'he' and híya 'she'. Thus, e.g. bíhaa 'with it (f.)' occurs in the 'Two Cats and a Monkey' fable, wáhwa (< wa+huwa, with the accenting of wa and elision of -u-) 'and he' potentially accented at line 3 of the passage 'The King and the Ancient' in Appendix A, and ?álaa (= interrogative particle ?a-+negative particle laa) three times in 'The Fishmonger's Sign' (also in Appendix A). It is noteworthy that the interrogative particle hal is regularly accented. The preceding cases of accented bi and wa, in particular, should be contrasted with the case of a following disyllabic form, e.g. bi Dǽrbah (< Dǽrbati) 'with a blow', wa 9álaa 'and on . . . ' The case of w@ qr@? 'and read' in the sentence ?únĐur jayyídan w@ qr@?! 'Look carefully and read!' in 'The Rewards of Reading' at the end of this chapter is interesting in that hamzátu lw@Sl and its vowel are properly elided from ?íqr@? 'read!' following wa, but the accent remains, so to speak, with the particle. In fact, wi, the Egyptian vernacular reflex of wa, is quite often accented in somewhat unexpected places and the fact that wa may be accented before húwa finds its vernacular parallel before e.g. da 'this (one), that (one)'.

Mention was earlier made of the high falling tone, but it has not so far been illustrated. It occurs twice, for example, in the conversational exchange under Sentence Practice in Sheet 5 of Appendix A. The onset of this tone is pitched above the level of preceding syllables, even when these include an accented syllable. Preceding syllables also tend to 'climb' from their valley to the peak provided by the tonal onset. The two examples in question are

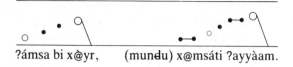

?ámsa bi x@yr,   (munĐu) x@msáti ?ayyàam.

The language involved in the first case is clearly that of the well-known Arabic sphere of polite inquiry and greetings, even with reference to a third person, to which the type of affective response illustrated, including the high fall, is appropriate. It is also noteworthy that the second example concludes the speaker's sentence and is an echo of the first example, with which the sentence opened. The feature may be marked by a vertical upward arrow, with the convention stated above, i.e. that preceding syllables usually 'climb' towards the syllable marked in this way. With the intra-linear transcription used for purposes of illustration, the arrow appears as follows: ?ámsa bi ↑x@yr and x@msáti ?ay↑yàam. I have, however, rarely found a need for the device in Appendix A.

It was noted in Chapter 7 that two syllabic structures are subject to accentual variation in Egyptian Classical pronunciation, and it was stated that this was attributable to difference of regional origin among speakers. Although this is overwhelmingly the case, it is not wholly so. The Azhari-trained Upper Egyptian speaker is particu-larly liable to fluctuate between paroxytonic and proparoxytonic

$$... \text{ or } \sharp/\text{\$}/\text{S}/Ł$$

and paroxytonic and hypertonic

$$... \text{ or } \sharp/\text{S}/\text{S}/\text{S}/Ł$$

(where ... indicates that the quantity of the relevant syllable is immaterial), as illustrated by qiT9ata and wajadataa in the text we have been exploiting. In a recording of the fable by an Upper Egyptian his clear tendency is to adopt Cairene paroxytonic accen-tuation for the two structures concerned when they occur at or near the beginning of sentences and sense-groups, when presumably recall of the accentual pattern of the word in isolation is strongest, but in the flow of the sentence, and *a fortiori* beyond the sentence, the tendency diminishes and the influence of Upper Egypt is much stronger. Perhaps more interesting, however, are those cases of fluctuation on the part of a speaker from Cairo or the Delta. These are very much rarer but do occur, and it is just possible that they reflect regional subdivisions within the Delta region. A speaker from Tanta, who regularly elsewhere produces paroxytones for the first of the two structures, nevertheless made proparoxytones of ǵ@@yati, kadaalika and saa9ati in Section D (Sentence Practice) of Sheets 5 and 7 ir Appendix A. Now it may be that this is due to regional influence, because accentuation does vary in some degree among the villages of the Delta, if not so much in the towns, but the last two examples at least may well be due to a more subtle form of 'vernacular influence', namely the very frequent occurrence of closely similar forms in everyday speech. The accentuation of familiar forms like kazáalik and sáaꬒa could easily be carried over into Classical performance. In the case of ǧ@@yah, I have noticed difference of treatment, perhaps sporadic, between fii ǧ@@yati ssaláamah 'in the utmost well-being', on the one hand, and ǧ@@yátun min@ SSíḥḥah 'the best of health', on the other, which may suggest a need to test the relevance of syllabification and rhythm in extended contexts and/or of grammatical category as well as regional provenance among the several factors which could contribute to such differences.[1] From the point of view of acceptability and intelligibility, the difference between ǧ@@yati and ǧ@@yátun does not, of course, matter greatly, but it has been felt useful to indicate an area in which the student, if the opportunity offers, might wish to pursue some early research of his own. It is to be expected that the type of variation in question is much more likely to appear in connected speech than in the word in isolation. In the two concluding passages below, as well as in the connected passages from *Writing Arabic* which conclude Appendix A, examples of the two variable patterns are marked with an asterisk.

There follows now the intonational-cum-accentual-cum-quantitative transcription of 'Two Cats and a Monkey' and 'The Rewards of Reading'. The student should try to obtain from different Arabic speakers their own versions of the passages and then compare them with the renderings given. These have been provided by two Azhari-trained speakers, one from Upper and the other from Lower Egypt, and it is Lower Egyptian practice that is followed in the transcription, with asterisked forms showing possible places of variation. Vertical lines indicate pauses made by the speakers.

Two Cats and a Monkey

hirr@táani *wajadátaa *qiT9á↓ta jùbn(in)
'Two cats found a piece of cheese

---

[1] It is also possible that the two patterns may provide the basis of some required rhythmical variation in connected speech.

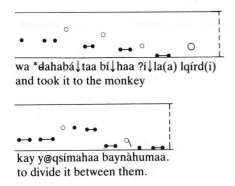

wa *ɖahabá↓taa bí↓haa ʔí↓la(a) lqírd(i)
and took it to the monkey

kay y@qsímahaa baynàhumaa.
to divide it between them.

fa ʔ@x@↓ɖa lqírdu l*jubnáta w@ *q@samá↓haa ʔílaa qismàyn(i),
And the monkey took the cheese and divided it into two parts,

ʔaɦadúhumaa *ʔakb@ru mina l?@@x@r(i). ʈumma w@D@ga
one of them bigger than the other. Then he placed

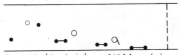

↓kulla *waaɦídin[1]↓mina lqismáyni[1]↓fii *kaffátin[1]↓min miizàanih(i).[1]
each (one) of the two parts in a pan of his scales.

f@ r@ja↓ɦa lqís↓mu l?àkb@r(u).
And the larger part weighed more.

---

[1] Notice the treatment of successive phrases of this sentence as single intonational items.

fa ?@x@↓da mínhu q@líilan bi *?asnaaníhi wa ?àkalah(u), w@ q@@l(a):[1]
So he took a little from it with his teeth and ate it, and said:

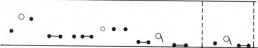

?uríidu ↓?an ?usaawíyahu bi l?@S¢@r(i). walàakin
"I want to make it equal to the smaller one." But

?id káana maa *?@x@dá↓hu mínhu *?akt@r@ mina lláazim(i),
since he took more than was (the) necessary from it,

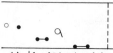

r@ja↓ha l?@S¢@r(u).
the smaller one weighed more.

fa fá9ala bi háadaa maa *fa9aláhu bi dàalik(a),
And he did with this what he had done with the other

wa maa záala *ya?kúlu ↓mimmaa[2] r@jaha mina lqismáyn(i)
and he went on eating from the heavier one of the two parts

hattaa ?ákala l*jubnáta *kullàhaa.
until he had eaten the whole piece of cheese.'

---

[1] Or q@@l (O_v).   [2] < min+maa.

The Rewards of Reading

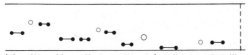

*?unŝí?at *jamϙiiyátun fii ?íh↓da(a) lmúdun(i)
'A society has been formed in one of the towns

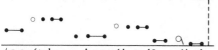

ǵ@@yátuhaa muħ@@r@batu l?ummìiyah.
with the object of fighting illiteracy.

fa fátaħat *haaɖíhi l*jamϙiiyátu *madaarísa *layliiyátan
This society has opened night-schools

fi(i) lqúr@@ wa lmúdun(i)[1]
in the villages and towns

li taϙlíimi lfallaaħíina wa lϙummáal(i)
for the purpose of teaching the peasants and artisans

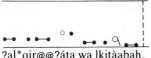

?al*qir@@?áta wa lkitàabah.
reading and writing.

---

[1] A fall–rise may sometimes be heard at such places as this, where it simply marks pause without any question of semantic contrast. The rise takes place, of course, on post-accentual syllables following the accented fall.

fa *?@rsá↓lat yáwman *mufattíśan ?ilaa ?íħ↓da(a) lqúr@@
One day it sent an inspector to one of the villages,

*yaħmílu hadáayaa li lladíina yataɡallamúuna
carrying gifts for those who were studying

fii *haadíhi l*madaarísi llaylíiyah taśjíi↓ɡan làhum.
in these night-schools, as an encouragement to them.

fa jtámaɡa ¹lfallaaħúu↓na ħáwlah(u)
The peasants gathered around him

wa dáɡa(a) ¹l*mufattí↓śu mr@?a↓tan mínhum
and the inspector called a woman from among them

w@ T@la↓ba mínhaa ↓?an *t@qr@?a *kalimátan
and asked her to read a word

?aśt@@r@ ?iláyhaa fii kitáab(in) káana fii yàdih(i).
which he pointed to in a book (that was) in his hand.

---

¹ It is noteworthy that the article is usually treated like other particles and involves a downward movement from a preceding vowel in order to mark the noun phrase of

f@ q@r@?at bi S@w↓tin 9ǎal(in): 'mindìil(un)'.
And she read in a loud voice: "Kerchief."

f@ q@@la láhaa: '?aħsànt(i)'. wa ?@9T@@haa mindìilaa.
And he said to her "Well done!" and gave her a kerchief.

tumma dá↓9aa r@julan w@ T@la↓ba mínhu
Then he called a man out and asked him

?an *y@qr@?a *kalimátan ?aś@@r@ ?ilàyhaa.
to read a word he pointed at.

f@ q@r@?a bi sǔr9ah:[1] 'ŧàwr(un)'.
So he hastily read out: "Ox!"

wa káanati l*kalimá↓tu śáy↓?an ?@@x@r(@).
But the word was something else.

f@ q@@la láhu lmufàttiś(u): '?únÐur *jayyí↓dan w@ qr@?!'
So the inspector said to him: "Look carefully and read!"

which it forms part. This correlation between intonational form and word (and phrase) divisions is an interesting feature of Arabic.

[1] Note the post-accentual rise.

fa n@Ð@↓r@ rr@julu *m@rr@↓tan ?úxr@@ w@ q@@l(a): 'ṫàwr'.
And the man looked again and said: "Ox!".

f@ q@@mat zawjátuhu w@ q@@lat: 'záwjii *yuḥsínu lqir@@?ah[2]
Then his wife stood up and said: "My husband can read well

*walaakinnáhu fii *ḥaajátin ?ilaa ṫáwrin *yaḥrú↓tu bí↓hi l?@rD(@).'
but he is in need of an ox to plough the land with."'

APPENDIX A

A.1 Pronunciation sheets[1]

The following eight sheets present the consonants and vowels of Classical Arabic in order of difficulty for the English-speaking learner. Those consonants which do not involve any special difficulty have not been singled out for particular attention. The book has not been presented as a teaching text and, in particular, to achieve proficiency in pronunciation, sentence practice is necessary from the beginning. The final section of each sheet is devoted to this purpose, and the material is associated with the intonational symbols explained in Chapter 8. The student should not proceed to a new sheet before mastering the previous one. Once the eight sheets have been completed, then the Reading Passages may be attempted. These have been taken from *Writing Arabic*, and the opening sura of the Quran has been added as an example of Quranic Arabic.

The learner may wish to record the material of the Appendix for the purpose of private study. If so, the speaker should be carefully chosen—an Egyptian without speech defect and with clear diction, preferably with the kind of Classical training on which this book is based. He should be carefully rehearsed before recording, and taught to use the same falling intonation on every word given, including those under Differentiation Practice, where the temptation for him will be to use contrastive intonation, with a rise or 'jump', or a mid-level tone for monosyllables, on the first member of the pair and a fall on the second. The use of contrastive intonation tends to distract from features on which the student is being asked to concentrate. The speaker must also ensure that a sufficient interval of time is left between the words and sentences of the several sections.

SHEET I

a. *Vowels* i, ii; a, aa

1. bi 'by, with'
2. min 'of, from'
3. bíhi 'with him/it'
4. fii 'in'
5. siin 'letter s'
6. siníin 'years' (obl.)
7. fa 'and, so'
8. man 'who'
9. ḏáhaba*[2] 'he went'
10. yaa (vocative particle)
11. baab 'door, chapter'
12. náama* 'he slept'

---

[1] Amended versions of those formerly used by me at SOAS.
[2] Non-pause forms are asterisked in individual words throughout the Pronunciation Sheets.

SHEET I

a. *Vowels*　　　　i, ii; a, aa

13. híya 'she'
14. yáfham 'he understands'
15. háadaa 'this (s.m.)'
16. haadíhi* 'this (s.f.)'

17. bináfs '-self'
18. fanaajíin 'cups'
19. mímmaa 'from which'
20. bíhaa 'with her'

21. záhaa 'it flourished'
22. jawaasíis 'spies'
23. jíizah 'Giza'
24. miizáanih 'his balance (genitive)'

b. *Consonants*　　?; geminated consonants

1. ?ajáaba* 'he answered'
2. ?ídaa 'if; and then'
3. ?ádina* 'he allowed'
4. ?ábaha* 'he heeded'
5. ba?s 'strength; harm'
6. ša? 'want!'
7. ?ási? 'harm!'
8. yá?nas 'he is sociable'
9. jáa?a* 'he came'
10. báa?a* 'he returned'

11. tanáa? 'praise'
12. jazáa? 'reward'
13. háni?a* 'he was delighted, he enjoyed'
14. haníi?an 'may you benefit!'
15. yáhna? 'he enjoys'
16. ?a?ímmah 'leaders'
17. bátta* 'he unfolded, he propagated'
18. šádda* 'he isolated, he stood out'

19. mássa* 'he touched'
20. házza* 'he brandished, he shook'
21. ?iwázz 'geese'
22. mánnaa 'he made s.o. want s.t.'
23. dámma* 'he blamed, found fault with'
24. hámma* 'he distressed s.o., he was about to (do s.t.)'

c. *Differentiation practice*

1. sinn 'tooth': siin 'letter s'
2. siin: šiin 'letter š'
3. ?aššáam 'Syria': ?aššáms 'the sun'
4. ?ána 'I': ?áana* 'time, moment'
5. ?ána: ?ánna 'that' (complementizer)
6. táman 'price': samn 'clarified butter'
7. samn: záman 'time, period'
8. ?itnáan 'two': fii ?atnáa? 'during'
9. bánaa 'he built: bannáa? 'builder'
10. ?ámma* 'he led in prayer': ?ámmaa 'as to, as for'
11. ?ámmaa: ?amáam 'in front of'
12. jaffáfa* 'he dried': jafráfah 'he dried it (m.)'

d. Sentence practice

1. háa ?àna ꝺaa ꞉ ꝺaahíban binàfsii. 'Here I am going alone.'

2. mannáa↓nii jámma jazáa?ih ꞉ wa naajíza ŧawàabih. 'He gave me cause to hope for complete and utter requital.'

3. yá?↓ba(a) ꝺꝺámma bi ?ánf in ?aśàmm. 'He haughtily (lit. with haughty nose) rejects (any) censure.'

4. maa máa↓na fámii ꞉ wa maa wáha↓na hàmmii. 'My mouth told no lie and my intent did not weaken.'

5. man sámaa bináfsih ꞉ fa maa bí↓hi ꝺàmm. 'God helps those who help themselves' (lit. 'whoever rises up by himself, no blame is upon him').

SHEET 2

a. Revision

1. ?in 'if'

2. miim 'letter m'

3. jahháza* 'he made ready'

4. jáhazaa 'they (dual m.) finished off s.o.'

5. śaabb 'young man'

6. maa? 'water'

7. mí?ah 'hundred'

8. ?aanása* 'he was friendly towards'

b. Vowels   u, uu; ay, aw

1. hum 'they (m.)'

2. jubn 'cheese'

3. ŧúmma 'then'

4. nuun 'letter n'

5. ?ayyúub 'Job'

6. ꝺuu 'endowed (with)'

7. ?uwáys (proper name)

8. báyna 'between'

9. háy?ah 'committee'

10. yawm 'day'

11. ?aw 'or'

12. ?awj 'summit; apogee'

13. munájjim 'astrologer'

14. yúusuf 'Joseph'

15. yúujib 'he enjoins (s.t. on s.o.)'

16. ?ayyúhaa (vocative particle)

17. húwa 'he'

18. samaawíiy 'heavenly (s.m.)'

19. muusawíiy 'Mosaic(al) (s.m.)'

20. mas?uumáan 'wearisome (dual m.)'

21. śu?úunii 'my affairs'

22. ?ayyáam 'days'

23. háwwaa 'he ventilated'

24. ?ijáazah 'permission; holiday'

c. Consonants   t, d

1. tíhta* 'you (s.m.) were lost; you were haughty'

2. túhmah 'accusation'

3. tiih 'wilderness; pride'

c. *Consonants*   t, d

4. támma* 'it was complete'

10. jadíid 'new (s.m.)'

16. dúmta* 'may you (s.m.) live long!'

5. tatíih 'you (s.m.) become lost; you show pride'

11. dabdábah 'tapping, pattering'

17. ?istiftáa? 'asking advice; referendum'

6. bátta* 'he cut off'

12. mufíid 'useful (s.m.)'

18. nabáat 'plant'

7. dáhama* 'he attacked (suddenly)'

13. tándam 'you (s.m.) regret'

19. wa?ádta* 'you (s.m.) buried alive'

8. jaddáda* 'he renewed'

14. túsdii 'you benefit s.o.'

9. dáydan 'custom, habit'

15. tadúum 'you (s.m.) continue'

20. tatadáawaa 'she *or* you (s.m.) treated s.o. medically'

d. *Differentiation practice*

1. tiin 'figs': diin 'religion'

2. núsiba* 'it was attributed to': nuusíba* 'he was of the same stock as'

3. nuun 'letter n': nawm 'sleep'

4. mu?ináyn 'two believers (obl.)': mu?miníin 'believers (obl.)'

5. sámada* 'he held his head high': saamáta* it (m.) faced (s.t.)'

6. yadíbbu* 'it (m.) creeps (into)': yatímmu* 'it is complete'

7. dam 'blood': damm 'censure'

8. támma* 'it was complete': támma 'there'

9. saah '(one) sheep, ewe': sáa?ah 'he wanted it (m.)'

10. báata* 'he spent the night': bátta* 'he cut (off)'

11. hádama* 'he demolished': haddáma* 'he blew up'

12. háwaa 'he fell': háwwaa 'he ventilated'

e. *Sentence practice*

1. yáa sabàab : há↓buu nnáfsa wa nnafíis : wa jídduu : fa man jád↓da wàjad. 'Young people, give the very best of yourselves and earnestly strive, for whoever seeks will find.'

2. jaa?ánii min ?ábii : nába?un saa?ànii. 'Distressing news has reached me from my father.'

3. ?áyna ssamáa?u mina lmàa?[1] 'There's the world of difference (between them)' (lit. 'where is the sky from the water?').

4. A: ?áyna tadhábu masàa?an? 'Where are you going this evening?'

---

[1] Strictly, l here occurs before its time on Sheet 3.

B: sayajii?ú↓nii ?ábii ⋮ wahwa yawáddu muṣaahádata ssìnamaa. 'My father is coming (to me) and would like to go to the cinema.'

A: ?á-wa ta?ḍánu bi ḍaháabii? 'Would you mind my going (lit. allow my going)?'

B: ?í↓ḍaa ṣi?t. 'If you like.'

SHEET 3

a. *Revision*

1. jawaasíis 'spies'

2. jíizah 'Giza'

3. miizáanih 'his scales' (gen.)

4. múujiz 'abridging'

5. mawt 'death'

6. ?itnáyn 'two (obl.)'

7. taamm 'complete (s.m.)'

8. dáffah 'rudder'

b. *Consonants*

l, r

1. laa (negative particle)

2. lii 'to me'

3. majlúub 'brought, imported'

4. law 'if'

5. jálaba* 'he brought, he imported'

6. silm 'peace'

7. salb 'pillage'

8. ?alláfa* 'he united; he composed'

9. sayl 'flood, torrent'

10. fiil 'elephant'

11. nafl 'work of supereroga- tion'

12. naḍl 'vile (person)'

13. r@?aa 'he saw'

14. ri?m 'white antelope'

15. ruṣd 'maturity' (of mind)

16. r@yy 'irrigation'

17. h@r@m 'senility; pyramid'

18. s@rr@b 'he sent in batches'

19. dars 'lesson'

20. bard 'cold'

21. sirr 'secret'

22. bi?r 'well'

23. fihr (proper name)

24. ?asr 'capture'

c. *Differentiation practice*

1. laháah 'uvula': láhaa 'to her'

2. ?aláan 'he softened': ?al?áan 'now'

3. laam 'he blamed; letter l': r@@m 'he desired'

4. ?íllaa 'except': málaa 'he walked briskly'

5. w@r@d 'he/it arrived': w@rr@d 'he got s.t. to s.o.'

6. ?asr 'capture': ?atl 'tamarisk'

7. ?alláa (< ?an+laa . . .) 'that not': ?@ll@@h 'God'

8. bi lláah 'with God': w@ ll@@h 'by God'

c. *Differentiation practice*

9. duhn 'oil': nahś 'biting, snapping'

10. múujiz 'abridging': múujaz 'concise'

11. dall 'he showed': tall 'hill'

12. báarid 'cold' (adj.): bard 'cold' (noun)

d. *Sentence practice*

A: háa↓ḏaa ↑ ?ànta yaa ?ibr@@hiim.[1] : hál tasallámta risaalátii? 'There you are, Ibrahim. Did you get my note?'

B: ?àjal.[2] : tasallamtúhaa munḏu zámanin wajìiz. : wa ?aasáfa↓nii s@f@ru lwaalídi lmufaají?i duuna ?an ?@r@@h. 'Yes, indeed. I had it a short time ago. I was sorry that your father left suddenly without my seeing him.'

A: láysa ṭammáta maa yuují↓bu l?àsaf, : fa sayá?tii ṭaaníyan fii haaḏa(a) śś@hr. 'There's no need for regret, because he's coming back again this month.'

B: wa ?íḏan fa sayasurrúnii ?an ?@r@@h, : wa ?ajlísa ?ilàyh. 'In that case I shall be delighted to see him and sit with him.'

SHEET 4

a. *Revision*

1. dáama* 'it lasted'

2. mas?álah 'problem, matter'

3. ?@hr@@m 'pyramids'

4. śay? 'thing; matter'

5. yáwbah 'he heeds'

6. bal '(not . . . .) but . . . '

7. ?@rr@?úuf 'the Merciful'

8. yuríid 'he wants'

b. *Consonants*   k, q

1. kátaba* 'he wrote'

2. kibr 'magnitude, grandeur'

3. kull 'each, every'

4. káana* 'he was'

5. kíila* 'it was measured'

6. kay 'so that'

7. kawn 'being; the universe'

8. ?adr@ka* 'he attained; he compre-hended'

9. ?akkáda* 'he assured'

10. ?úktub 'write!'

11. ?ak?ába* 'he saddened'

12. sá?alak 'he asked you (s.)'

13. q@ttála* 'he massacred'

14. qism 'part, division'

15. qul 'say!'

---

[1] After a high–fall on ?an-, pronounce the remaining syllables on a low level monotone, but relative quantities must still be respected.

[2] nágam would be more natural, but 9 is not illustrated before Sheet 6.

16. q@@ma* 'he stood'

17. qíila* 'it was said'

18. q@yl 'princeling, chieftain'

19. q@wl 'speech; saying'

20. d@qíiq 'thin, delicate (s.f.)'

21. d@qq@q 'he pulverized; he was meticulous'

22. w@r@quk 'your (s.) papers'

23. ?úqtul 'kill!'

24. b@qq 'bug(s)'

c. *Differentiation practice*

1. kíila* 'it was measured': qíila* 'it was said'

2. kawm 'heap': q@wm 'people'

3. kun 'be!': qum 'stand up!'

4. káana* 'he was': q@@ma* 'he stood up'

5. kátaba* 'he wrote: káđaba* 'he lied'

6. r@qm 'numeral': r@kb 'cavalcade'

7. láaq@@ 'he met': láakaa 'they both chewed'

8. śakk 'doubt': ś@qq 'crack, rent'

9. ?áana* 'time': káana* 'he was'

10. q@h@r 'he conquered': máhal 'he dawdled'

11. kád@r 'muddiness; sadness': q@d@r 'destiny'

12. nákada* 'he pestered': n@q@da* 'he paid in cash'

d. *Sentence practice*

q@@la mu?ađdíbu l?amíiri li l?amíiri đaata yáwm: : '?a t@r@@ haađíhi l?iwazzáta wa ?awlaadáhaa? : hum láhaa surúur : wahya láhaa wiq@@yah.' : fa btásama l?amíiru wa ?awmá?a bi r@?sih. : q@@la lmu?àddib: : 'kađáalika[1] takúunu li ?ummátik : wa kađáalika takúunu ?ummátu↓ka làk.'

'One day the prince's tutor said to the prince: "Do you see this goose and her young? They are her joy and she is their protection." The prince smiled and nodded his head. The tutor said: "Thus are you to your people and they to you."'

SHEET 5

a. *Revision*

1. ś@r@@b 'drink'

2. hámma* 'he distressed; he was about to (do s.t.)'

3. q@@saa 'he underwent'

4. m@r? 'man'

5. bádalan mín 'instead of'

6. káfaa 'it was enough'

7. t@mr 'dried dates'

8. suu? 'evil'

[1] See pp. 129–30.

SHEET 5

a. *Revision*

9. haddáda* 'he threatened'

10. sáaq@* 'he drove'

11. zawj 'husband'

12. rífq@h 'company'

b. *Consonants*   x, ǵ

1. x@bíit 'bad; repulsive'

2. xíftu* 'I feared'

3. xusr 'loss, damage'

4. x@@dim 'servant'

5. xíifa* 'he was feared'

6. xuubír@* 'he was written to'

7. x@ybah 'failure'

8. x@wf 'fear'

9. náf@x@* 'he blew'

10. ta?ríix 'dating; history'

11. y@xdim 'he serves'

12. ǵayx 'sheikh, elder'

13. ǵ@f@r@* 'he forgave'

14. ǵírr@h 'heedlessness'

15. ǵúrfah 'room'

16. ǵ@@yah 'aim; end'

17. ǵ@saq@ 'twilight' (accus. def.)

18. masǵúul 'busy; processed'

19. ǵ@yr 'different from; not, non-'

20. ǵíilah 'assassination'

21. ǵuǵl 'work; being busy'

22. balíiǵ 'eloquent'

23. m@ǵrib 'west'

24. sáb@ǵ@* 'he dyed'

c. *Differentiation practice*

1. háadim 'devastating': x@@dim 'servant'

2. káamil 'complete': x@@mil 'unknown; languid'

3. lukh 'chew it (m.)!': ruxx 'roc; rook (chess)'

4. x@riba* 'it went to ruin': ǵ@ruba* 'it set (of sun)'

5. x@@ba* 'it failed': ǵ@@ba* 'he was absent'

6. ǵ@ǵ@ba* 'he rioted': ǵ@r@ba* 'he drank'

7. q@fr 'desert, wasteland': ǵ@fr 'forgiveness'

8. xiláal 'bit (of drill), skewer': qiláal 'summits'

9. rux@@m 'marble': rukáam 'heap (sand, clouds, etc.)'

10. sákana* 'he lived, dwelt; it abated': s@qima* 'he became ailing'

11. rusǵ 'wrist': xusr 'loss'

12. ?@xdah 'action of taking (once)': b@ǵtah 'surprising happening'

d. *Sentence practice*

A: masáa↓?u lx@yri yaa x@@lid. ⋮ káyfa ?axùuk? 'Good-evening, Khalid. How's your brother?'

B: ?ámsa bi ↑x@yr ⋮ wa laq@d x@r@ja li nnuzháti li ?awwá↓li m@rr@h ⋮ mund̪u x@msáti ?ay↑yàam. 'Better this evening. He's gone out for a walk for the first time in five days.'

A: háa↓d̪aa x@yr. ⋮ g̪@yr@ ↓?annii ?@r@@ ↓?alláa yusrífa fi(i) lxurúuj ⋮ f@ q@d tasúu?u lm@g̪@bbah. 'That's good. But it just seems to me that he shouldn't go out too much or it may have a bad effect.'

B: láa t@x↓ṣa d̪àalik ⋮ fa haad̪aa r@?yu dduktùur. 'Don't worry about that. It's the doctor's advice.'

A: sa?azuurú↓hu g̪@dan fi(i) lx@@mísati g̪@@lìban ⋮ wa ?@rjuu ↓?an yakúuna fii g̪@@yati[1] ssalàamah. 'I shall visit him at 5 o'clock tomorrow, probably. I hope he'll be quite better then.'

SHEET 6

a. *Revision*

1. y@g̪ris 'he plants'

2. ?ist@g̪r@q@* 'he was immersed in'

3. f@?r 'mouse'

4. fa?ínna 'because'

5. g̪@yru q@líil 'not too few'

6. s@qíim 'ailing'

7. x@ríif 'autumn'

8. sáaxin 'hot, warm'

9. q@ríib 'near'

10. káatib 'clerk, writer'

11. jadíid 'new (s.m.)'

12. s@xx@r@* 'he subjected'

b. *Consonants* ḥ, 9

1. ḥámal 'he carried; lamb'

2. ḥilm 'gentleness'

3. ḥúmur 'donkeys'

4. ḥáalim 'dreamer'

5. ḥíika* 'it was woven'

6. ḥuubíya 'he was sided with'

7. suḥáym 'blackness'

8. r@ḥḥába* 'he welcomed'

9. r@ḥmah 'pity; kindness'

10. náfḥah 'breeze; present'

11. r@@ḥa* 'he went'

12. riiḥ 'wind'

13. 9ámal 'action'

14. 9ilm 'knowledge'

15. 9umr 'life; age'

16. 9íisaa 'Jesus'

17. fá9ala* 'he did'

18. fa99ála* 'he scanned (verse)'

19. ba9l 'Baal; husband'

20. ?isti9dáad 'preparedness'

[1] See pp. 129–30.

b. *Consonants*　　　　　　ħ, 9

21. rúq9ah 'patch;　　22. sáb9ah 'seven'　　　　23. sibáa9 'beasts of
piece of paper;　　　　　　　　　　　　　　　　prey; lions'
calligraphic　　　　　　　　　　　　　　　　24. r@w9 'alarm'
style'

c. *Differentiation practice*

1. háamid 'calm; extinct': ħáamid　　7. nábaha* 'he is famous':
'lauding'　　　　　　　　　　　　　　nábaħa* 'it barked'

2. ħáamil 'carrying': x@@mil　　　　8. naħl 'bees': n@xl 'palm-trees'
'unknown; languid'

3. 9áamil 'doer, worker': ħáamil　　9. r@?y 'opinion': r@9y
'carrying'　　　　　　　　　　　　　'protection, care'

4. nafħ 'exhaling fragrance;　　　　10. ta?míir 'investing with
presenting with': naf9　　　　　　　authority': ta9míir
'benefit, use'　　　　　　　　　　　'(re)construction'

5. 9áabir 'crossing, passing over':　11. ?abúuh 'his father': ?abúuħ 'I
ǵ@@bir 'past, ancient'　　　　　　　reveal a secret'

6. ?isti9m@@r 'colonizing;　　　　　12. lujúu? 'taking refuge': rujúu9
exploitation': ?istiǵf@@r　　　　　　'returning'
'asking forgiveness'

d. *Sentence practice*

1. ?al9íl↓mu 9ín↓d@ ll@@h. 'God knows.'

2. ?ist@ǵ@@ta wa laa muǵiit. 'He cried for help but no helper came.'

3. ?al9íl↓mu núurun wa ljáh↓lu 9@@r. 'Knowledge is light and ignorance
is shame.'

4. ?alħílmu sayyídu l?@xl@@q. 'Forbearance is the prince of virtues.'

5. ħáa↓dir 9áma↓la ssùu?. 'Beware of evil-doing.'

6. ?al9ádlu ħamíidu l9@@qìbah. 'Fair dealing is of happy outcome.'

7. A: ?assaláamu 9alàykum. 'Peace be upon you!'
B: wa 9aláykumu ssaláamu w@ r@ħmá↓tu ll@@hi wa b@r@kàatuh.
'Peace and the mercy and blessings of God be upon you!'

8. ?aħíbba li ?axíika maa tuħíbbu li nàfsik. 'Do unto others (lit. your
brother) as you would have others do unto you (lit. what you like for
yourself).'

SHEET 7

a. *Revision*

1. fátħah 'vowel a;　　2. mu9állim　　　　3. ħim@@r 'donkey'
an opening'　　　　　　'teacher'

4. lawḥ 'board, blackboard'

5. 9iyáadah 'clinic; doctor's visit'

6. x@laaxíil 'anklets'

7. x@la9a* 'he took off'

8. jaḥš 'young donkey'

9. layl 'night(-time)'

10. musta9ídd 'prepared'

11. ?@ǵl@q@* 'he foreclosed (e.g. on mortgage)'

12. fiir@@n 'mice'

b. *Consonants*

S, Ḍ

1. S@f@r@* 'he whistled'

2. Sifr 'zero'

3. Suudíq@* 'he was treated as a friend'

4. m@Síir 'development, progress'

5. S@yr 'happening'

6. f@S@@ḥah 'eloquence'

7. ?@@Sír@h 'bond, tie'

8. f@Sl 'severance; chapter'

9. ?@Sǵ@r 'smaller (s.m.)'

10. q@miíS 'shirt; amice'

11. múxliS 'sincere, devoted'

12. luSúuS 'robbers'

13. Ḍ@h@r@* 'it appeared'

14. Ḍuhr 'noon'

15. Ḍ@@nn 'thinking, believing'

16. Ḍann 'opinion, view'

17. Ḍ@lla* 'he went on doing s.t.'

18. 9@Ḍíim 'great, mighty'

19. ḥáfiḌ@* 'he preserved, he guarded'

20. y@Ḍh@r 'he/it appears'

21. w@@Ḍib 'persevere!'

22. maḥfúuḌ 'preserved, guarded'

23. n@ḌḌ@m 'he put in order'

24. tahfííḌ 'memoriza-tion, inculcation'

c. *Differentiation practice*

1. S@laba* 'he crucified': sálaba* 'he stole'

2. ?assíin 'the letter s': ?@SSíin 'China'

3. S@@n 'he preserved': S@ff 'row, line'

4. fasíiḥ 'roomy': f@Síih 'eloquent; literary'

5. ḥiSn 'fortress': ḥusn 'beauty'

6. m@nSúur 'victorious': m@nḌúur 'visible'

7. Ḍ@lla* 'he went on doing s.t.': dálla* 'he showed, he indicated'

8. ḍáhab 'gold': Ḍuhr 'noon'

9. Ḍuhr 'noon': Ḍ@h@r 'he appeared'

10. taḥáffuz 'preparedness': taḥáffuḌ 'caution'

11. 9@@Ḍ@l 'he was repetitious': 9áaḍil 'critic, censurer'

12. r@?aa 'he saw': r@9aa 'he pastured, he tended (flock)'

d. *Sentence practice*

A: S@báa↓ħu lx@yri ↓yaa S@làaħ : ?@ S@@dáfta ?ibr@@híim? 'Good-morning, Salaah. Have you come across Ibrahim?'

B: nàgam. : laq@d káa↓na húnaa mundu ħíinin ŧumm@ nS@r@f. 'Yes. He was here a while ago but went off.'

A: ?a t@Đúnnu ?annáhu sayagúudu fii háad@(@) SS@báaħ? 'Do you think he will be back this morning?'

B: láa ?@Đún↓nu đàalik. : walaakínnii sa?uq@@bíluhu bagd S@láa↓ti ĐĐùhr. 'I don't think so, but I shall meet him after the noon-prayer.'

A: ?ínnii ?ant@Điru wuSúul@ S@díi↓qii Súbħii li ziy@@r@tii : wa ?@rjuu ↓ ?an tuṡarrífa↓nii ?ánta wa ?ibr@@híim : bi tanaawúli lg@dáa↓?i màganaa. 'I am waiting for the arrival of my friend Subhii, who is coming to see me, and I hope that you and Ibrahim will honour me by taking lunch with us.'

B: ṡúk↓r@n làk. : waláakin y@Đħ@ru lii ↓?anna ?ibr@@híima galaa màwgid. : fa ?ín¹ ↓lam yákun kađáalik : fa sa?@Sħábuhu ?ilaa manzílika fi(i) ssáagati² lwaaħídati wa nníSfi bagd@ ĐĐùhr. 'Thank you, but I have an idea (lit. it seems to me) that Ibrahim has an appointment. If that isn't so, I'll come with him to your house at half-past one this afternoon.'

SHEET 8

a. *Revision*

1. lág9ab 'he made s.t. play'	5. ħ@ĐĐ 'good luck; fate'	9. r@xíim 'soft, mellow'
2. tawr 'bull'	6. đáaq@* 'he tasted'	10. S@xr 'boulders'
3. dars 'lesson'	7. r@bb 'master, lord'	11. S@ħħáħa* 'he cured; he rectified'
4. ħ@SS@l 'he obtained'	8. ṡáari9 'street'	12. muSíibah 'misfortune'

b. *Consonants*   T, D

1. T@9áam 'food'	5. T@wwaf 'he walked around'	8. mabsúuT 'contented'
2. Tiin 'clay'	6. r@Tl 'pound' (weight)	9. b@TT@la* 'he thwarted'
3. T@yr 'birds'	7. murtábiT 'connected; bound (by)'	10. núqT@h 'dot, full stop'
4. Tuul 'length'		

¹ May be pronounced ?il before following l.   ² See pp. 129–30.

11. f@q@T 'only'

12. qíT9ah 'piece'

13. D@r@ba* 'he hit, he struck'

14. D@yf 'guest'

15. Du9f 'weakness'

16. Diiq 'narrowness'

17. ?@D9áaf '-fold' (as 'twofold', 'hundredfold', etc.)

18. ?iDT@r@ba* 'he got excited'

19. D@lla* 'he lost his way'

20. tafwíiD 'commissioning, authorizing'

21. muDíif 'host'

22. ?@rD 'earth'

23. q@D@@? 'decision, judgement'

24. 9@DD@da* 'he supported'

c. *Differentiation practice*

1. tiin 'figs': Tiin 'clay'

2. tábi9a* 'he followed': T@ba9a* 'he stamped, sealed'

3. T@yy@@r 'flying; pilot': tayy@@r 'current, stream'

4. r@Tíib 'moist': r@tíib 'monotonous'

5. śáamit 'malicious': śámiT 'he turned grey'

6. dálla* 'he demonstrated': D@lla* 'he lost his way'

7. D@lla* 'he lost his way': Đ@lla* 'he went on doing s.t.'

8. d@rb 'pass; alley': D@rb 'beating'

9. w@D@9 'he put down': wádda9 'he bade farewell'

10. mufíid 'useful': tafwíiD 'authorizing'

11. s@@r 'he set out': S@@r 'he became'

12. sayf 'sword': S@yf 'summer'

d. *Sentence practice*

1. ?íD↓ḥak y@D↓ḥak lá↓ka l9áalam ꞉ wá b↓ki táb↓ki wàḥdak. 'Laugh, and the world laughs with you; weep, and you weep alone.'

2. maa D@@↓9a ḥ@qqun w@r@@?áhu muT@@lib. 'A rightful possession which has a claimant is not lost.'

3. laa y@Tíi↓bu DD@n↓ku ?íllaa li D@9ìif. 'Only the weak acquiesce in the lowly life.'

4. T@@ba masàa?uk. 'Good-evening', or 'May your evening be (a) pleasant (one).'

5. Dúriba D@rbá↓ta làazib. 'He met with disaster.'

6. T@nT@@ 9@@Símatu m@nTíq@ti l&́@rbiiyáti bi mìSr. 'Tanta is the chief city of the western zone of Egypt.'

7. ?innáhu S@@ḥí↓bu ḥáwlin w@ T@̀wl. 'He is indeed a man of power and might.'

8. A: ?a tuTríbuka lmuusíiq@@? 'Does music please you?'

B: nàgam. ⦙ tuTríbunii wa tahúz↓zu q@l↓bii báyn@ Dulùu9ii. 'Yes, it delights me and moves me deeply (lit. shakes my heart between my ribs).'

A.2 Reading Passages

With the exception of the opening sura of the Quran, which concludes the section, the following eight passages, like those at the end of Chapter 8, have been taken from *Writing Arabic* and, in turn, from J. Kapliwatzky's *Arabic Language and Grammar*.

Ahmad and the Sailor

sá?ala *?aħmádu[1] mallàaħan: ⦙ '?áy↓na máata ?abùuk?' ⦙ fa ?ajáaba lmalláaħ: ⦙ 'fii *m@rkábin kaana y@rkábuhu fi(i) lb@ħr.' ⦙ 'wa ?áy↓na máa↓ta jàdduk?' ⦙ 'hú↓wa ?áy↓D@n máata fii *m@rkábin kaana y@rkábuhu fi(i) lb@ħr.' ⦙ 'wa ?án↓ta láa tax@@fu ↓?an *t@rkába *m@rkában ba9da ðáalik?' ⦙ f@ q@@la lmallàaħ: ⦙ '?áy↓na máata ?abùuk?'[2] ⦙ '9alaa fir@@śih.' ⦙ 'wa jàdduk?' ⦙ '9alaa fir@@śih.' ⦙ 'wa ?án↓ta láa tax@@fu ↓?an tanáama 9ala(a) lfir@@śi ba9da ðáalik?'

'Ahmad asked a sailor: "Where did your father die?" The sailor answered: "On a ship he was sailing on the sea." "And where did your grandfather die?" "He, too, died on a ship he was sailing on the sea." "And aren't you afraid to sail a ship after that?" Then the sailor said: "Where did *your* father die?" "In his bed." "And your grandfather?" "In his bed." "And aren't you afraid to sleep in a bed after that?"'

The Fishmonger's Sign

fáta↓ħa r@julun dukkáa↓na sámak ⦙ wa *9all@↓q@ fáwq@ *baabí↓hi láwħan S@ǵíi↓r@n kútiba 9alàyh: ⦙ 'húnaa yubáa↓9u ssàmak'. ⦙ fa jáa↓?a ?áħadu ?@Sdiq@@?ih : w@ q@@↓la làh: ⦙ 'limáaɖaa katábta 9ala(a) lláwħi *kalimá↓ta "hùnaa"? ⦙ ?álaa yubáa↓9u ssáma↓ku ?íllaa fii dukkáanik?' ⦙ fa ħáɖafa *S@@ħíbu ddukkáani *kalimáta 'hùnaa'. ⦙ ŧumma jáa?a S@díi↓qun ?@@x@r : f@ q@@la li *S@@ħíbi ddukkáan: ⦙ 'limáaɖaa katábta 9ala(a) lláwħi *kalimáta "yubàa9"? ⦙ ?álaa *yafħá↓mu nnáasu ↓?annaka láa *tuwazzí↓9u ssámaka majjáanan?' ⦙ fa ħáɖafa *kalimáta 'yubàa9'. ⦙ ŧumma jáa?a S@díi↓qun ŧáaliŧ ⦙ w@ q@@l: ⦙ 'limáaɖaa katábta

---

[1] Forms of structure (. . ./)S/S/Ł and S/S/S/Ł are, of course, variable as to accentuation, and will often be heard accented respectively on S and on the first S-syllable. They are indicated by a preceding asterisk.

[2] Preferably with a contrastive high–fall, i.e. '*your* father as opposed to *mine*'.

*kalimá↓ta "ssámak"? : ?álaa y@r@@↓hu nnáas : wa láa yaśummúunah?'
: fa názaga *S@@ħíbu ddukkáa↓ni llàwħ.

'A man opened a fish-shop and hung above its door a small board on
which was written: "Fish Sold Here". One of his friends came and said to
him: "Why have you written the word 'Here' on the board? Is fish sold only
in your shop?" So the shopkeeper erased the word "Here". Then came a
second friend and said to the shopkeeper: "Why have you written the word
'Sold' on the board? Don't people understand that you don't give fish out
free?" So he erased the word "Sold". Then a third friend came and said:
"Why have you written the word 'Fish'? Don't people see it and smell it?"
So the shopkeeper took down the board.'

The King and the Ancient

r@↓?aa máli↓kun śáyx@n *waaħídan *y@ǵrí↓su n@xlaa : w@ q@@↓la
làh: : '*?ayyú↓ha(a) śśàyx! : ?a *tu?ammílu ?an *ta?kúla min támari
háada(a) nn@xl : wahwa láa *yutmí↓ru ?íllaa bagda siníina katíir@?' : f@
q@@↓la śśàyx: : '*?@ǵrí↓su nn@xla li *ya?kúla ?aħfáadii min támarih :
kamaa ?akál↓tu ?ána mimmaa ǵ@r@↓sa jàddii.' : fa *staħsá↓na lmáli↓ku
dàalik : wa ?@9T@@hu giśríina diin@@r@n. : fa *?@x@dá↓ha(a) śśàyx :
w@ q@@l: : '*?ayyú↓ha(a) lmàlik! laq@d ?akál↓tu ?ána bináfsii min támari
háada(a) nn@xl.' : fa *tagajjá↓ba lmáliku min kaláamih : wa ?@9T@@hu
giśríina diin@@↓r@n ?ùxr@@. : fa *?@x@dá↓ha(a) śśàyx : w@ q@@l: :
'*?ayyú↓ha(a) lmàlik! wa *?agjábu min kúl↓li śáy? : ?anna nn@xla q@d
*?atm@↓r@ ssánata m@rr@tàyn.' : fa *tagajjá↓ba lmáliku min *kalaamíhi
wa ?@9T@@hu giśríina diin@@↓r@n ?ùxr@@.

'A king saw an old man planting a palm-tree and said to him: "Sheikh, do
you hope to eat the dates of this palm when it will not bear fruit for many
years?" Said the old man: "I am planting the tree so that my grandchildren
may eat of its dates just as I myself ate of those my grandfather planted."
This pleased the king, who gave him twenty dinars, and the old man, taking
them, said: "Behold, O King, I have myself already eaten of the fruit of this
palm." And the king marvelled at his words and gave him a further twenty
dinars, which the old man took, saying: "O King, the most wondrous thing
of all is that the palm has already borne fruit twice this year." And the king
was amazed at his words and gave him yet twenty dinars more.'

Man and Death

ħáma↓la r@julun *m@rr@tan *ħuzmá↓ta ħ@T@bin mina l*ǵ@@báti
l*q@riibáti ?ilaa báytih : fa t@qulat galàyh. : fa lám↓ma tágiba min
*ħamlíhaa : r@↓maa bíhaa gan kátifih : wa dágaa galaa *nafsíhi bi lmàwt. :
fa ś@x@S@ lá↓hu lmàwt : w@ q@@l: : 'háa ↓?ana dàa! : limáadaa

daɣawtànii?' ⫶ f@ q@@↓l@ rr@jul: ⫶ 'daɣawtúka li tuhammílanii *huzmá↓ta lh@T@bi *haadíhi ɣalaa kàtifii.'

'A man once carried to his tent from the nearby forest a bundle of wood which weighed heavily upon him. When he tired of carrying it, he threw it from his shoulder and called Death down upon him. Death appeared to him and said: "Here I am! Why indeed have you called me?" Said the man: "I called you to load this bundle of wood on to my shoulder."'

Appearances Deceive

káana S@yyáadun y@Síidu ɣ@S@fíir@ fii yáw↓min báarid ⫶ fa káana yadbáhuhaa wa ddumúuɣu tasíilu min ɣaynáyhi min *śiddá↓ti lbàrd. ⫶ f@ q@@↓la ?áhadu lɣ@S@fíiri li *S@@híbih: ⫶ 'laa t@x@f min háa↓d@(@) rr@jul! ⫶ ?álaa t@r@@↓hu yábkii?' ⫶ f@ q@@↓la lá↓hu l?@@x@r: ⫶ 'laa t@nDur ?ilaa dumúuɣih ⫶ bal ?ílaa maa *t@Snáɣu yadàah.'

'A hunter was out hunting and slaughtering sparrows on a cold day, and the tears were streaming from his eyes from the extreme cold. One sparrow said to his companion: "Do not fear this man! Don't you see he's weeping?" But the other said to him: "Look not at his tears but at what his hands are doing."'

The Talking Parrot

káana li r@julin bab@ǵ@@?u jamíilah ⫶ *taɣrífu lkalàam. ⫶ wa ?í↓daa m@r↓r@ bí↓haa r@ju↓lun q@@↓lat láh: ⫶ '*nah@@ruka saɣíid ⫶ yaa ?@xii.' ⫶ wa káanat *t@xrúju ?ila(a) lbustáani baɣd@ DDúhr ⫶ wa tant@Diru S@@híba↓haa ?ílaa ?an *y@rjíɣa min dukkáanih ⫶ wa *ɣindámaa t@r@@↓hu káanat t@qúul: ⫶ 'yaa ɣámmii ⫶ xúdnii ?ila(a) lbàyt.' ⫶ f@ D@@ɣati lbab@ǵ@@↓?u yáwman ⫶ fa káana S@@híbuhaa *yas?á↓lu kúl↓la nnáa↓si ɣanhaa ⫶ f@ q@@↓la lá↓hu ?áhadu rrijáal: ⫶ '?innii samíɣ↓tu S@wta bab@ǵ@@?a fii báy↓ti j@@rii.' ⫶ fa dáhaba *S@@híbu lbab@ǵ@@?i ?ilaa j@@↓ri *dáali↓k@ rr@jul ⫶ wa *sa?aláhu ɣani lbab@ǵ@@?. ⫶ fa lám↓ma sámi↓ɣat S@wta S@@híbi↓haa q@@lat: ⫶ 'yaa ɣámmii ⫶ xúdnii ?ila(a) lbàyt!' ⫶ fa d@x@↓l@ rr@julu wa *?@x@dáhaa min báyti ssàariq.

'A man had a pretty parrot which knew how to speak, and whenever a man passed by her, she would say to him: 'Good day, brother." She would go out into the garden in the afternoon and wait for her master to return from his shop, and when she saw him, she said: "Take me home, uncle." One day the parrot was missing, and her master was asking everybody about her when a man told him: "I heard a parrot's voice in my neighbour's house." The parrot's owner went to the man's neighbour and asked him about the parrot. And when she heard her master's voice she said: "Take me home, uncle." So the man went in and took her from the thief's house.'

Attempted Car Theft

?alqùds: : lám↓m@(@) qt@r@ba *ssayyí↓du fáa? min ?áħadi śabaabíi↓ki
d@@rih : r@?aa ?anna sayy@@r@tahu lw@@qífata ?amáa↓ma lbáyt : q@d
rúfiɡa↓ti[1] stiɡdáadan li ?@xđi ?iT@@r@@tiħaa. : fa *?@xb@r@ fi(i) lħáali
*m@rkáza lbuulíisi bi đàalik. : f@ x@ffa rijáalu lbuulíisi ?ilaa makáani
lħàadiŧ. : *walaakinnáhum lam *yaɡŧúruu ɡalaa ?áħadin bi qúrbi
ssayy@@r@h. : wa láa yazáalu ttaħqíiqu mustamìrr@n.

'Jerusalem: When Mr F. went to one of the windows of his house, he saw
that his car, standing in front (of the house), had been jacked up in
preparation for the removal of its tyres. He immediately informed the
police station and policemen rushed to the scene of the incident. But they
discovered no one in the vicinity of the car, and the investigation is (still)
continuing.'

Lebanese Aircraft Purchases

*?alq@@hìr@h: : *wikaalátu l?anbáa?i lɡar@bìiyah: : *satabdá?u
*śarikátu TT@y@r@@ni *llubnaaniiyátu *ɡamaláhaa fii *?awaaxíri
haađa(a) śś@h↓ri lmùqbil. : w@ q@di śt@r@t ŧaláaŧa ɡáś@r@t@[2]
T@@?ír@tan *tijaariiyátan min *biriT@@niyaa : w@ x@msa T@@?ir@@tin
min ?amríikaa : li n@qli rrukkáabi bayna lubnáana wa l?@qT@@ri lɡar@bìiyah. : wa *sataɡqídu *śśarıká↓tu[3] ttif@@qiiyáatin maɡa śarikáa↓ti[3]
TT@y@r@@ni l*?amriikiiyáti wa lbiriT@@níiyah : li n@qli *rukkaabíhaa
?ilaa ?uurúbbaa wa ?amríikaa wa bi lɡàks. : wa hunáaka *ɡiddátu
śarikáatin *lubnaaniiyátin li TT@y@r@@n : tamma láhaa lħuSúulu ɡala(a)
tt@rxíiS : wáh↓ya l?áana *taɡmálu fii ?iijáadi TT@@?ir@@ti
l*m@Tluubá↓ti làhaa.

'Cairo: The Arab News Agency:
The Lebanese Aviation Company will begin operations at the end of this
coming month, and has already bought thirteen commercial aircraft from
Britain, and five aircraft from America, for the transport of passengers
between the Lebanon and the Arab countries. The Company will conclude
agreements with American and British aviation companies for the con-
veyance of its passengers to Europe and America and back. And there are a
number of Lebanese aviation companies who have obtained authorization
and are now busy obtaining the aircraft requested for them.'

---

[1] The anaptyctic vowel may be regarded as belonging to the following word from
the point of view of accentuation. This applies also to word-final case vowels before
hamzátu lw@sl, notably in the case of the article. The vowel often carries a descent in
pitch serving to mark the beginning of the following word.

[2] ɡáś@r@ta (not ɡáś@r@ta) in this and similar compound numerals is treated
differently from elsewhere, and regularly occurs with the accent as shown.

[3] Here again the case vowel carries a descent in pitch before the article.

The 'fatíihah' or opening sura from the Quran

The principles of Quranic chant or even recitation have been proclaimed as beyond the scope of this book. For present purposes, use a very deliberate style of enunciation, carefully maintaining the ratio between short, medium and long syllables, and especially between short and long vowels, of which the latter are, in fact, often noticeably protracted. Plosive consonants occurring before pause should be accompanied by considerable tenseness of articulation but released slowly and with deliberation, whereas continuants[1] in the same context should not be cut short. Level pitch, at about the middle of the voice range, is usual in pause, with some variation in height. In the main, pausal syllables tend to echo one another.

bi smi lláahi rr@ḥmáani rr@ḥíim. ː ?alḥámdu li lláa↓hi r@bbi lɡaalamíin,
ː ?@rr@ḥmáani rr@ḥíim, ː máali↓ki yáw↓mi ddíin, ː ?iiyáaka *naɡbúdu wa
?iiyáaka nasta9íin, ː ?ihdín@ SSir@@T@ lmust@qíim, ː Sir@@T@ lladíina
?anɡámta 9aláyhim, ː ǧ@yri lm@ǧDúubi 9aláyhim, ː wa lá↓@ DD@@llíin.[2]
ː ?áamíin.[3]

'In the name of Allah, the Compassionate, the Merciful. Praise to Allah, Lord of the worlds, the Compassionate, the Merciful, Master of the Day of Judgement. Thee we worship and to Thee we cry for help. Lead us to the right path, the path of those to whom Thou hast been gracious, not of those with whom Thou art angry nor of those who have lost their way. Amen.'

A.3 'Vernacular influence'

It seems useful at this point to pull together briefly the principal features which, in various chapters of the text, have been said to distinguish a high Classical from a more relaxed reading style. The latter is characterized by 'vernacular influence', and is manifested most markedly by

(i) the elimination of 'heavy emphasis' in favour of backness;
(ii) the greater spread of backness (e.g. muh@@r@b@ for muh@@-r@bah or muhaar@bah). This is accompanied by a relaxation of the principle by which the consonant opening a syllable exerts the greatest influence on the quality of a following vowel;
(iii) the omission of final -h of the táa? m@rbúuT@h ending;
(iv) the use of long vowels, generally speaking, only in (*a*) accented, and (*b*) open syllables, with the exception of pre-pausal -CVVC;

---

[1] i.e. sounds which may in theory be indefinitely prolonged.
[2] The final syllable is especially drawn out. Pronounce it on a somewhat lower pitch than the preceding mid-level pausal syllables, and on the same level as D@@l-.
[3] Both syllables are greatly protracted. Pronounce them on the same pitch and as an echo of the preceding D@@llíin.

(v) the use of s, z and Z for ṱ, ḍ and Ḍ, except in certain lexical items;

(vi) the use of g for j;

(vii) the somewhat sporadic use of ? for q, which is a shibboleth of Classical pronunciation. In some lexical items, q is in any case obligatory;

(viii) the relaxation of semivowel pronunciation, so that -ay- and -aw- may take the form of diphthongs proper;[1]

(ix) for rare cases of fluctuating accentuation which are very possibly due to vernacular influence, see pp. 129–30. It should be remembered that this influence is much more likely to arise in connected speech than in the isolated word.

---

[1] Monophthongization of -ay- and -aw- in the form of vernacular -ee- and -oo- does not belong to Classical pronunciation proper, and it may be remarked in passing that, even in vernacular Arabic, -ay- and -aw- may not be monophthongized in certain structures and classes, cf. mawgúud 'present', láyla 'Leila' (contrast léela 'night'), sáwsan 'Susan', etc.

APPENDIX B

BRIEF GLOSSARY OF ARABIC PHONETIC TERMS

The following list, to which the student may add as his work progresses, is owed to W. H. T. Gairdner,[1] with the exception of the terms of vowel description, which have been taken from the introductory material of Hinds and Badawi's *Dictionary of Egyptian Arabic*.[2]

phonetics	9ílmu *m@x@@ríji lħurúuf (lit. 'science of the outlets of the letters')
place of articulation	m@xr@j (lit. 'outlet')
consonant(s)	ħ@rf/ħurúuf (lit. 'letters')
vowel(s)	ħ@r@kah/ħ@r@káat (lit. 'movement(s)')
lengthening	?almádd
lengthened	mamdúud
unvoicing or voicelessness	hams (lit. 'whispering')
unvoiced or voiceless	mahmúus (lit. 'whispered')
voice or voicing	j@hr
stop consonants	ħurúufu śśíddah or ?alħurúufu śśadíidah (lit. 'the tense consonants')
continuant consonants	ħurúufu rr@x@@wah or ?alħurúufu rríxwah (lit. 'the slack or lax consonants')
rolled or trilled consonant	ħ@rfun *muk@rr@r@h (lit. 'reiterated consonant')
roll(ing) or trill(ing)	takríir
lateral	śajaríiy
sibilants or sulcals	ħurúufu SS@fíir or ħurúufu tt@Sfíir (lit. 'the whistling consonants')
throat	?alħ@lq
back of throat (= larynx)	?@qS@(@) lħ@lq
middle of throat (= pharynx)	wás@Tu lħ@lq
front of throat (= back of velum or uvula)	?ádna(a) lħ@lq

[1] W. H. T. Gairdner, *The Phonetics of Arabic* (London, OUP, 1925), 106–7.
[2] Martin Hinds and El-Said Badawi, *A Dictionary of Egyptian Arabic* (Beirut, Librairie du Liban, 1986), p. xvii.

guttural	ḥalqíiy
uvula	?allaháah
palate	?alḥánaku l?áglaa (lit. 'the highest palate') or s@qfu lḥának (lit. 'the roof of the palate')
back of palate	?@qS@(@) lḥának
middle of palate	wás@Tu lḥának
alveolum	?allítah (lit. 'the gum')
tongue	?allisáan
back of tongue	?@qS@(@) llisáan
middle of tongue	wás@Tu llisáan
blade of tongue	r@?su llisáan
side of blade (or rim)	*ḥaafátu r@?si llisáan
top of blade (dorsum)	Ð@hru r@?si llisáan
point or tip of tongue	T@r@fu llisáan
lingual	lisaaníiy
teeth	?al?asnáan
molar(s)	Dirs/?@Dr@@s
bicuspid(s)	Ð@@ḥik/Ð@wáaḥik
canine(s)	naab/?anyáab
lateral incisor(s)	rubaagíiyah/rubaagiiyáat
front incisor(s)	ŧaaníiyah/ŧanáayaa
lip(s)	śáfah/śafatáan
labial	śafahíiy or śafawíiy
backing or emphaticization (of open vowel or of consonant)	tafxíim
back or emphatic consonants	?alḥurúufu l*muf@xx@mah (lit. 'the dignified consonants')[1]
full emphaticization	?iTb@@q (lit. 'lidding')
fully emphatic consonants	?alḥurúufu l*muTb@q@h (lit. 'the lidded consonants')
fronting or non-emphaticization (of open vowel or of consonant)	t@rqíiq
front or non-emphatic consonants	?alḥurúufu rr@qíiq@h or ?alḥurúufu l*mur@qq@q@h (lit. 'the delicate consonants')
back open vowel (i.e. @)	fátḥah *muf@xx@mah
front open vowel (i.e. a)	fátḥah *mur@qq@q@h
front close vowel (i)	kásr@h *x@@líS@h (lit. 'pure kásr@h')
back close vowel (u)	Ð@mmah *x@@líS@h
front mid vowel (i.e. vernacular ee)	kásr@h mumáalah

---

[1] i.e. T, D, S, Ð, (Z), q, r, x, ǵ and l of ?@ll@@h.

back mid vowel (i.e. vernacular oo)   Ḍ@mmah mumáalah

closing (sometimes also fronting) of   ?imáalah (lit. 'inclination', i.e.
   fátḥah   towards kásr@h)[1]

---

[1] This refers, for example, to the occurrence at times of a closer quality of a in the context of kásr@h in an adjoining syllable.

INDEX OF TOPICS AND TERMS

INDEX OF SYMBOLS

Symbols are presented as far as possible in the order of the roman alphabet. 9 and ?, however, are included after Z. Square brackets enclose IPA symbols where appropriate.

Note: The IPA length mark [:] also appears on pp. 41, 41 f. n. 1, 42, 43, 53, 57, 75.

Consonant Symbols (*cont.*)